Using Cases To Improve College Teaching

A Guide To More Reflective Practice

by
Pat Hutchings

A publication of
The AAHE Teaching Initiative
American Association for Higher Education

The Author

Pat Hutchings is director of the AAHE Teaching Initiative at the American Association for Higher Education. Before joining AAHE, she was a faculty member in the English Department at Alverno College, in Milwaukee; she continues to teach, part-time, at the University of Maryland University College.

USING CASES TO IMPROVE COLLEGE TEACHING
A Guide To More Reflective Practice
by Pat Hutchings

© 1993 by the American Association for Higher Education. All rights reserved. Printed in the United States of America.

A publication of the AAHE Teaching Initiative. For more about AAHE and its Teaching Initiative, see page 89.

Additional copies of this publication are available for $15.00 each for AAHE members; $17.00 each for nonmembers. Bulk discounts and express delivery are available. For ordering information, contact:

AMERICAN ASSOCIATION FOR HIGHER EDUCATION
One Dupont Circle, Suite 360
Washington, DC 20036-1110
phone 202/293-6440, fax 202/293-0073

TABLE OF CONTENTS

v   **Preface**

1   **Chapter I:**   **Cases About College Teaching and Learning: A Picture of Emerging Practice**
An overview of how faculty currently are using cases to improve teaching and learning, with a preliminary look at the kinds of cases that work for this purpose, and five reasons to try cases on your campus.

7   **Chapter II:**   **The Case for Cases: A Deeper Rationale**
A look at principles and assumptions underlying the use of cases, focusing particularly on the match between cases and a conception of teaching as substantive, scholarly activity.

13   **Chapter III:**   **Using Cases on Your Campus: Three Examples, and Strategies for Making Them Work**
A description of the case-discussion method, followed by three actual cases, from different settings and disciplines, with "teaching notes" and suggestions to help you use them successfully on your campus.

41   **Chapter IV:**   **Writing Cases on Your Campus**
Reports from two groups of faculty who have written cases about teaching and learning in their own settings, including the benefits of doing so and suggestions for how to proceed.

47   **Chapter V:**   **Achieving the Promise of Cases: Next Steps and Emerging Issues**
Nine issues that have emerged through the use of cases thus far, with commentary suggesting next steps in this evolving field.

53   **Chapter VI:**   **Cases and Campus Culture**
Three possible scenarios of how cases might contribute to a campus culture that takes teaching and learning seriously.

59   **Appendix A**   **References: Sources Cited in Text or Boxes**

61   **Appendix B**   **Resources: Projects, People, and Materials**

67   **Appendix C**   **Additional Cases: With Teaching Notes**
Four more cases for campus use, with teaching notes.

89   **Appendix D**   **About AAHE**

PREFACE

Six years ago, at AAHE's National Conference, K. Patricia Cross called on audience members to "take teaching seriously." Today, on campuses across the country, efforts are under way to do just that.

New approaches to teaching and learning are capturing the attention of growing numbers of faculty. Strategies for collaborative and cooperative learning are changing the way students and faculty interact in the classroom; the assessment movement and the practice of Classroom Research are helping faculty ask important questions about who their students are and how they learn best. Moreover, beyond new strategies and methods, there's a growing recognition that what's really needed to improve teaching is a campus culture in which good practice can thrive, one where faculty talk together about teaching, inquire into its effects, and take collective responsibility for its quality. This monograph argues that *cases* can be a powerful route to developing such a culture.

Cases are not new, of course. They have a long-established place in law and business education, where they are both carriers of the "stuff" of the field and vehicles for teaching it. In social work and psychology, cases and case study are a recognized form of research and professional inquiry. In teacher education, work is under way to develop and use cases as curricular materials, and several volumes of such cases are now available. But with a few exceptions (most notably the work of C. Roland Christensen at Harvard University), the potential of cases for helping faculty learn how to teach has gone largely unexplored. What is that potential? How might cases help campuses "take teaching seriously"?

In the summer of 1990, with funding from Lilly Endowment Inc., AAHE launched a three-year project to begin answering these questions. Our aim was to develop cases about college teaching and learning in a variety of disciplines — materials that could be used to open up the traditionally private world of the classroom to collaborative, reflective discussion among faculty.

Much of the first year of the project was spent talking with people in fields that historically have used cases to good effect, learning the features of the genre, thinking hard about how cases would "play" in the larger world of college teaching. Many of the ideas in this monograph come especially from our interactions with the almost 1,000 faculty who have attended AAHE workshops on the use of cases and helped us test and refine our early hypotheses. Many of those faculty now have written cases about teaching on their own campus, sharing them with us and colleagues elsewhere, planting the seeds for an important new discourse about college teaching and learning.

Now, as the project moves into its final stage, we're eager to build on what has been accomplished so far. With an ever-growing collection of cases, there's an emerging need to develop (at AAHE or elsewhere) a systematic clearinghouse for cases about college teaching and learning; this, in turn, means working with faculty who have been writing and using cases in order to establish standards and criteria for quality — a process that was begun in October 1992 at an AAHE case authors retreat in Airlie, Virginia. We're particularly excited now, too, about our work with faculty who are developing cases that focus on how students learn — and, therefore, how teachers should teach — key concepts in the disciplines, e.g., the concept of acceleration in physics, of social stratification in sociology, and so on. Such cases constitute what Ernest Boyer has called "the scholarship of teaching" and could appear in the scholarly journals of the disciplines. Raising the status of teaching in the disciplines is, we believe, a key step in raising the level of attention to it, and its quality, on campus.

In the meantime, this monograph is intended as an interim report on AAHE's project on cases; it's also an invitation to participate. Toward that end, we've tried to make the chapters that follow both thoughtful and practical, with sufficient "how-to" and guidance about using and writing cases to get you started on your own campus. You'll find an argument for cases; several deliberately varied examples, with notes about using them; and suggestions for beginning your own case-writing venture. Appendices include information about projects around the country that complement the work reported here, and also several additional cases. Feel free to use and adapt whatever you find useful; then let us know what you're doing, what you're learning, and how AAHE can help.

We want to extend a special thanks to Lilly Endowment Inc. for generous support of this monograph and the project it draws on. We're grateful, as well, to the many colleagues across the country who have helped us sharpen our sense of how cases can make a difference in the quality of teaching and learning and who have generously shared their time and expertise.

Russ Edgerton
President, AAHE

Pat Hutchings
Director, AAHE Teaching Initiative

CHAPTER I

CASES ABOUT COLLEGE TEACHING AND LEARNING
A Picture of Emerging Practice

In the winter of 1991, when my AAHE colleague Ted Marchese was invited to a Midwestern state university to lead a workshop on "active learning," he decided to try out the first product of AAHE's then-new project Cases About College Teaching and Learning. That case, designed to prompt in-depth discussion of (and "active learning" about) pedagogical issues, recounts a carefully planned day in "Dr. Susan Green's" introductory history class. As the case begins, Dr. Green is in mid-sentence, giving an assignment about the "mythopoeic method," when an otherwise quiet student calls out from the back of the room, "I thought this was supposed to be a history class!" As the case unfolds, it is clear that Dr. Green and her students have quite different ideas about what it means to study history.

After the ninety-five faculty, students, and administrators assembled for Ted's workshop had read the three-page account of Dr. Green's class, he began, "You're the teacher. You've just finished the class session featured in this case, and you sit down with colleagues in the cafeteria for lunch. What do you tell them about what happened?" After a few seconds, a faculty participant in the front row answered, "Nothing . . . we don't talk about our teaching."

But, in fact, over the next hour there was lively, energetic exchange about the case: about the incident it portrays, people's different "readings" of the incident, and strategies for dealing with such situations. It seemed that people not only were willing to talk about teaching but were full of good ideas and eager to talk some more, to hear further from one another, to keep the conversation going . . . as *cases* can.

What Is a Case?

That scenario suggests several of the key aspects of the conception of cases described in this monograph: that is, cases that *depict incidents of teaching and learning* in order to *raise pedagogical issues and prompt discussion of them.* (Our focus, then, is not the kind of "curricular case" that might be used to transmit content to students in the classroom.) As in the above scenario, the audience for cases about college teaching and learning might include students and administrators, but first and foremost *these cases are intended for faculty*, whether in interdisciplinary or department-based groups, casual brown-bag lunch discussions or extended retreats, in groups of four, forty, or one hundred. Most such cases are in written form, though videotaped cases, while expensive to produce well, have a special kind of power; many are three or four pages long, but I've seen wonderful cases ranging all the way from one-paragraph vignettes to thirty and forty pages. In the midst of all this variety, however, it's possible to point to four features shared by cases likely to prompt more reflective teaching.

A first feature is **authenticity**. Cases prompt serious discussion and reflection when, and only when, faculty find them believable, life-like, realistic. This is not to say that cases must be literal accounts of actual incidents, though they might be; it *is* to say that the characters, situations, and dilemmas described must ring true, for faculty readers will be quick, says veteran case writer William Welty, to "smell contrivance." Seen from the point of view of the case writer, the issue is not "real vs. fiction" but rather how to select and represent experiences so as to prompt meaningful discussion of teaching and learning.

Concrete detail is a second feature of cases that work. Concreteness helps create authenticity, but its importance also lies in the fact that teaching does not occur in a vacuum. As Kenneth Eble noted, "it is attention to the particulars that brings any craft or art to a high degree of development" (1988, p. 6). So too with teaching — and it's the capacity of cases to represent the particulars of who's teaching what, to whom, under what conditions, that makes them powerful in raising pedagogical issues.

For most readers, the power of cases lies in large part in their **narrative form**. This is not to say that cases must read like short stories; one of the examples reproduced in Chapter III, for instance, is organized more around data about students than around a central protagonist with whom we identify. Nevertheless, cases engage our attention for some of the same reasons a piece of fiction does: We read to watch the action unfold, to find out what happens next, often identifying with the actors, feeling personally involved in their choices, playing out the consequences.

Finally, cases work when they're **open-ended**. Long-time Harvard case writer Abby J. Hansen speaks of cases as having an "irreducible core of ambiguity" (Christensen 1987, p. 56). Complex and information-rich, cases depict teaching and learning incidents that are deliberately

---

A Case Is...

"From the writer's point of view, I would describe a case as an account of real events that seem to include enough intriguing decision points and provocative undercurrents to make a discussion group want to think and argue about them."
(Hansen in Christensen 1987, p. 265)

"[Cases provide] a forum for presentation and critical examination of theoretical principles and alternative approaches, which take into consideration the constraints and complexities of a classroom situation. Using cases as the basis of deliberation and analysis provides opportunities for teachers . . . to test their knowledge of theory with practice."
(J. Shulman 1990, p. 76)

"The goal [of case discussion] is what Roland Christensen terms 'education for judgment.' Ideally that means [that] participants arrive at informed judgments that integrate a complex array of perspectives."
(Washington Center "Casebook," p. 3, see Resources)

open to interpretation — raising questions rather than answering them, encouraging problem solving, calling forth collective faculty intelligence and varied perspectives, and promoting more reflective practice.

How Are Cases Being Used?

The power of cases to prompt more and better talk about teaching is an idea that's taking hold in a variety of settings for a range of purposes. (Several of the examples that follow are described in more detail in Resources in the Appendix.)

At Eastern Michigan University, faculty in a number of departments have begun using cases to solve problems they face with their own students. In the math department, for instance, student underpreparation has been a persistent issue, the subject of ongoing hallway conversation. But most of that conversation, department members told me during a campus visit, has been "unproductive moaning and groaning." Seeing cases as a way to focus the conversation and move it to a more productive level, math faculty have begun writing cases about their own classes to discuss with colleagues at Friday afternoon department meetings.

In other settings, cases are being used to explore more cross-cutting pedagogical issues. At Pace University, Rita Silverman and William Welty have support from the Fund for the Improvement of Postsecondary Education (FIPSE) to develop what eventually will be a set of thirty cases about diversity issues in the classroom. A dozen such cases are now complete and have been discussed by faculty groups in a variety of settings. (One is reproduced in Chapter III.) The details of the discussion change with the group (that's part of the fun *and* the strength of cases), but what's clear across settings is the power these cases have to help faculty talk about issues of race and gender that otherwise might seem too thorny to touch.

In the state of Washington, cases are being used not only to explore an issue but to advance an important educational idea. Through the Washington Center for Improving the Quality of Undergraduate Education, an interinstitutional consortium founded at Evergreen State College, a faculty group recently has developed and begun using a set of cases focused on their work in collaborative "learning communities." Cases, they're finding, provide an appropriately interactive way to invite other faculty, as well as students and administrators, to participate in and advance collaborative teaching and learning.

Not surprisingly, some campuses are developing and using cases with new teachers in mind. At the University of Maryland University College, the discussion of a case about the first night of class has been part of an orientation and training session for adjunct faculty for several years. More recently, at Northwestern University and the University of Texas at Austin, cases have been introduced to help teaching assistants strategize about problems they commonly face in the classroom.

New teachers were also the intended audience for a set of cases about the teaching of writing developed under the auspices of the Alliance for Undergraduate Education, a consortium of sixteen public research universities. But in workshop settings where the cases have been discussed, their power to engage faculty at *all* levels of experience has become clear. The idea, as one of the five faculty authors explained to me, is to pose common problems in the teaching of writing in a way that will help people solve them in their own context. (An interesting footnote here, suggesting other, nondiscussion-based ways that cases might be used: Chris Anson, one of the case authors and director of the writing program at the University of Minnesota, recently has proposed that the program's instructors do written analyses of the cases to include as an entry in their teaching portfolios.)

Perhaps the longest-standing and most well known use of cases about teaching and learning is at Harvard University, in the seminar on college teaching developed and taught by C. Roland Christensen. A pioneer of case-method teaching in the Harvard Business School, Christensen saw the method's potential for helping Harvard Business School faculty develop their teaching skills. Gradually, however, the seminar was joined by faculty from across the university, and it continues today under the auspices of the Derek Bok Center for Teaching and Learning.

What Makes Cases So Powerful?

The next chapter looks at a "deeper rationale" for cases, with special attention to the case itself and its features as a genre. But at the risk of putting cart before horse, it's possible, on the basis of activities and projects such as those just described, to say a few things about the *discussion* of cases and why those discussions can be so powerful.

One reason is that **good cases are just plain interesting**: They tell a story, involving us in particular settings with particular people whose problems we puzzle over, debate about, and "relate to." Not everyone is as enthusiastic as the faculty member in an AAHE case workshop who explained, "This is the best discussion of teaching I've had in twenty years!" But even skeptics of "faculty development" find it hard not to get caught up in the *discussion* of teaching and learning when cases are the prompt.

A second reason is that **cases put permission in the air** for faculty to talk openly about their teaching. Cases provide an occasion for faculty to share experiences and expertise — and this at a time when many faculty have twenty-plus years in the classroom to draw on. "Cases have helped us realize the expertise that faculty on this campus have," says a faculty member from Florida Community College at Jacksonville (a campus featured in Chapter IV). But cases also make it possible for faculty to reveal uncertainty, frustration, and failure. Permission to do so comes, as one faculty member working with AAHE noted, because case discussion is "non ego-invested." The conversation starts not with *my* teaching but with *someone else's*; the invitation is out to think aloud and try out new ideas, in what Bill Welty and Rita Silverman describe as the "learning laboratory" provided by a good case. The risk is low, the benefits high.

A third reason to try cases is that faculty involved in a case discussion about teaching are, along the way, learning **a method they can try out** in their own classrooms. The pedagogy of the case method is active learning at its best, and many faculty who have attended AAHE's workshops on cases about teaching and learning have been quick to see the potential for cases in their own classroom, used to teach key concepts in more lively, active ways. Not incidentally, biology professor Clyde Herreid, author of one of the cases reproduced in Chapter III, also has written a case (available from AAHE) about *using cases* with his students at SUNY Buffalo. And some would

> ## A Silence in Need of Breaking
> "In this respect teaching was exactly like sex for me — something you weren't supposed to talk about or focus on in any way but that you were supposed to able to do properly when the time came. And the analogy doesn't end there. Teaching, like sex, is something you do alone, although you're always with another person/other people when you do it; it's hard to talk about it to the other while you're doing it, especially if you've been taught not to think about it from an early age. And people rarely talk about what the experience is really like for them, partly because, in whatever subculture it is I belong to, there's no vocabulary for articulating the experience and no institutionalized format for doing so."
>
> *(Tompkins 1990, p. 656)*

argue that it's in the classroom that cases and the case method of discussion will do their most important work when it comes to the improvement of teaching.

Fourth, **cases create a sense of community** where, for most teachers, isolation has ruled the day. Following a case discussion among some 100 colleagues from the Vermont state colleges, one participant wrote me a note saying, "It was wonderful to hear how thoughtful and caring my colleagues are about teaching." Faculty participating in the Washington Center project on cases report a similar satisfaction ("You may leave the session not only more impressed by your colleagues but liking them more, as well") and also note how, in well-run discussions, "the community intelligence evolves" (Washington Center "Casebook," pp. 4-5, see Resources). Such comments bring to mind current concerns about the reward system for teaching, reminding us that promotion, tenure, and merit pay are not the only coin in town. The experience of being part of something bigger that matters, the feeling of colleagueship, the sense of collective responsibility and efficacy . . . these too are rewards that faculty value and that cases can deliver.

Finally, **cases make sense because they fill a gap**. There's an exciting array of new (or newly interesting) methods and approaches that faculty today are experimenting with in their own classrooms: Classroom Research, collaborative and cooperative learning, experiential learning, service learning. The number of conferences and publications for learning about such strategies seems ever on the rise. But while new techniques are important, something larger may be more needed: habits of inquiry into teaching and learning, regular occasions for informed conversation about it, and a sense of collective responsibility for the education students receive. What's needed, in short, and what cases can help create, is a change in culture.

CHAPTER II

THE CASE FOR CASES
A Deeper Rationale

Cases have a special power to get people talking with one another about teaching — trying out ideas, trading points of view, sharing stories, being energized, and (not incidentally) having fun doing it. Such outcomes are, I suspect, sufficient reason for trying cases on many campuses, where the level of conversation about teaching is low to nonexistent. But there's a deeper rationale for cases, as well, one that begins not with the fact of good discussion but with cases themselves as a genre particularly well matched to emerging conceptions of effective teaching.

A View of Teaching as Technique

Efforts to improve teaching thrive or fail, at least in part, depending on how faculty *think about* teaching. The view of teaching varies from campus to campus and from person to person, but judging from institutional policies and procedures on many campuses, teaching appears to be seen mainly as a matter of *technique* and *method*. Most evaluation of teaching looks primarily at process; programs aimed at the improvement of teaching typically focus on the need for new and better "instructional technology," more up-to-date tools and strategies for, say, active learning, the use of small groups, employing computers. . . . These are important subjects, and good teachers want and need to know about method and technique.

However, where a technique-oriented view of teaching falls short is in failing to encourage a conception of teaching as substantive, intellectual activity — a shortfall with serious repercussions. If teaching is mostly a matter of technique, it is not, after all, a subject requiring serious, scholarly attention and inquiry. Whereas research is "work" (as in "*real* work"), teaching is a "load." As such, it is a topic unlikely to be talked about and debated in sustained, deliberate ways; there may be war stories told in the stairwells, but organized public occasions for discussion of teaching are rare indeed.

> "The road to a richer view of teaching, it seemed, might lie in shifting the focus from the general to the particular."
>
> *(Edgerton 1991, p. iii)*

Worst of all, a view of teaching as disembodied technique simply doesn't wash with faculty: Parker Palmer, author and teaching consultant (and a frequent presence at AAHE events) tells the story of a faculty member who approached him at the beginning of a workshop he had been invited to lead on a campus he was visiting. "Look," the faculty member said in a surly sort of way, "I teach organic chemistry. If you're going to tell me that I have to use 'role playing,' I'm leaving this workshop right now."

Unfortunately, a focus on methods and technique disembodied from particular subject matter and particular students' learning of it has predominated in the way we talk when we talk about teaching, and that diminishes teaching by portraying it as unconnected to the knowledge and values faculty most care about, unconnected to intellectual life, even to student learning, and therefore unlikely to be the subject of serious inquiry and improvement. What's needed for improvement is a view of teaching that lends itself to serious, collegial discussion and reflection.

A View of Teaching as Scholarship

An important step toward such a view was taken in the 1990 report from the Carnegie Foundation for the Advancement of Teaching — now one of its best-ever sellers — *Scholarship Reconsidered: Priorities of the Professoriate*. In it, Ernest Boyer argues for a broader conception of scholarship, one that includes not only traditional research (the scholarship of discovery) but a scholarship of application, a scholarship of integration, and — most to the point here — "a scholarship of teaching." Boyer actually says very little about the nature of this final category, but the high level of interest in it on campuses today speaks to its power to put a more promising conception of teaching into our thinking.

What would that conception look like in practice? What would it mean to view teaching as a scholarly activity? An answer I frequently hear is that faculty might begin writing scholarly articles about their teaching — not a bad idea in moderation. But seeing teaching as a scholarly activity has deeper implications, three of which bear comment here in the context of cases.

A first implication is that teaching would be seen not just as process (method and technique) but in terms of its substance or content. The disjuncture between the process and content of teaching is long standing, as issues of pedagogy have been relegated to schools of education and issues of content firmly housed in the chemistry (or wherever) department. To talk about teaching as scholarship is to call for a reconvergence, as Stanford University professor of educational psychology Lee Shulman has been doing for a number of years now in positing what he calls "a pedagogy of substance." The best teachers, Shulman contends, are those who can transform key concepts in their field for particular student audiences through a repertoire of metaphors, analogies, and examples. "Lee's message is this," writes AAHE president Russ Edgerton, "To appreciate the rich complexities of teaching, teaching that really produces understanding, we must go beyond general methods, get *inside* the subjects being taught, and look closely at the particular pedagogies that might be used to transform these subjects into terms the students can understand" (1990, p. 16). It's at this juncture of what is being taught to whom that the scholarship of teaching manifests itself.

A second implication of a scholarly view of teaching would be *epistemological*; that is, that teaching as scholarship entails not only the delivery of knowledge but the *generation* of it. On one level, this can mean having new insights arise in the midst of teaching: I think of something about T. S. Eliot I've never thought of, perhaps because of something a student says, or because the sun is shining on the floor in a certain way. But more significantly, the point is that teaching itself is something that is learned through *doing* it, and that the kind of knowing and expertise one needs to do it effectively is largely an experiential knowing, a wisdom achieved through practice and reflection upon it.

This insight needs to be held up against the orthodoxy of academe, in which theory (carefully posited and tested through research) holds the privileged place, and practice is assumed to be a secondary, derivative kind of activity. But recent work on professional expertise in teaching suggests quite a different balance: Good teachers don't learn the theory and then trot off to their classroom to apply it; rather, practice *informs* and *generates* theory. This dialectic between theory and practice is essential to the work of what Donald Schön calls "the reflective practitioner," for whom "we have recast the relationship between research and practice." To call for a "scholarship of teaching" is to call for the kind of reflective practice in which "research is an activity of practitioners" (1983, p. 300).

The third implication of the "teaching as scholarship" view is simple but essential: that teaching would be public. One of the things most of us have in mind when we think of scholarship, after all, is work that contributes to a larger corpus and is available for others to examine, critique, and further refine — a state of affairs far from achieved for teaching on most campuses today. I think here of a remark made by a faculty member who attended AAHE's special Forum on Exemplary Teaching, which is dedicated to good talk about teaching: "To talk publicly about one's teaching as if it were meaningful is to embarrass oneself," she observed in a reflective piece for *Change* magazine. "It's like discovering at a formal dinner that you're eating someone else's salad" (Gillespie 1989, p. 57). To say that teaching is scholarship is to suggest that talk about teaching will be not only socially acceptable but professionally expected. Peer review will be something we get good at, rather than something we deny can be done.

> "Case method faculty development [approaches] teacher training not from a theoretical point of view, but from the point of view of the practitioner, the teacher. It is a pedagogy based on inductive reasoning which constructs a theoretical base for college teaching by reflecting upon the individual actions of real college teachers."
>
> *(Silverman and Welty 1991, p. 4)*

A scholarly view of teaching, to sum up, would mean a view of teaching that is not just method, but method conjoined with intellectual substance; not just the delivery or application of knowledge, but the genesis of it; and not private, but public and collegial. Those are big changes, unlikely to be fully realized in the short term, but they are also the very changes that cases can help effect . . . as illustrated, I think, by the following story.

A Case in Point

Recently, I was visited by Deborah DeZure, codirector of the Faculty Center for Instructional Excellence at Eastern Michigan University and, like me, a teacher of literature and composition. Deborah was interested in cases, and we were talking about the draft of a case I had written about teaching John Updike's often-anthologized short story "A&P" in an introductory literature class (the case, "Tried and True," appears in Additional Cases in the Appendix). In the case, the all-female class balks at the story, which begins when three young women in swimsuits, described in great and adoring detail by the young male checkout clerk who narrates the piece, come into the local supermarket. "The author is sexist!" students angrily insist, and suddenly the teacher's plan to discuss the formal elements of literature has a considerable wrench thrown into its works.

"Well," said Deborah (who was giving me feedback for a revision of my draft), "this case is certainly familiar. It's the dilemma most English teachers have over and over: You want students to 'relate' to the literature, but you want them to be able to exercise some critical distance, too." My guest found the teacher's goals in the case (which were clearly on the "critical distance" end of the continuum) "perfectly appropriate . . . but what happens," she went on, "is that the teacher fails to set the stage. . . ."

In no time at all, my colleague and I (for that is what we had quickly become) were swapping stories about how, in fact, one *might* set the stage, why Updike's often-taught story is hard for students, what strategies a teacher could use to put things on a productive track, how the scenario in the case might be different with men in the class. "What *I* do when I teach this story," Deborah went on, "seems sort of theatrical but it really works. I go out into the hall after the first few minutes of class, cover myself with a sheet, and return. 'Now, who can remember what I was wearing?' I ask students. In no time at all, they begin to see how difficult it is to be observant, how differently men and women observe, how hard it is to describe what you see. I've found that this exercise goes a long way toward helping students understand the narrator of the story and Updike's special talents as a writer. They still don't like it when we're forced to dwell, paragraph after paragraph, on the girls' swimsuit-clad bodies, but they understand and appreciate the narrator more deeply — and they're more prepared to 'go with the story'."

We went on to talk about how one would adapt Deborah's idea to a group of older students, and how indeed it might go wrong in some settings. We talked some more about teaching women as opposed to men, and about whether traditional formalist frameworks were still useful for achieving our goals in teaching literature, or whether the promise lay with one or another more contemporary approach, and on and on for considerably longer than we had originally intended.

I have taught Updike's "A&P" a number of times over the years; I was a faculty member for nine years at an institution that talked more about teaching than just about any place I can imagine. Still, my discussion with Deborah DeZure was one of the richest exchanges I've ever been part of. What we had been talking about was not, it's important to say, simply a trick for introducing "A&P"; we were having a scholarly exchange about a scholarly activity, and we were having it because of a case.

> "Unlike professions such as architecture and law, where previous practice is accessible through such means as blueprints and legal casebooks, teachers' work is more ephemeral, and, partly as a consequence perhaps, not so valued."
>
> *(Ingvarson and Fineberg 1992, p. 2)*

The Case for Cases

That exchange was, first, an exchange at precisely the intersection of process and content being explored through Shulman's concept of pedagogical content knowledge. Deborah and I were not, as I say, talking about a technique for starting discussion. We were analyzing the fundamental problem, learning-wise, that Updike's story poses for a particular group of students; we were looking for ways to understand that problem, and ways to address it, that fit the details of the situation. A powerful argument for cases is, then, their ability to situate the conversation about teaching in this middle ground between process and content (or technique and substance), where a particular teacher, with particular goals, teaches a particular piece of literature (in this instance), to particular students. It's worth repeating Kenneth Eble's quote from the first chapter: "It is attention to the particulars that brings any craft or art to a high degree of development."

Second, cases uncover and recognize the legitimacy of the wisdom of practice. At the end of our hour-and-a-half discussion of "Tried and True," Deborah and I both had said things we hadn't said before, articulated knowledge we had been only partly conscious of. Donald Schön has written about the "knowing-in-action" that expert practitioners possess, and there's a growing literature about teachers' wisdom of practice. But the fact is that on most campuses, there is little occasion for faculty to express that wisdom or publicly to test out tacit knowledge. Cases provide such an occasion. In their open-endedness, cases invite faculty to give voice to what they know, to think aloud about classroom issues, to share their approaches to common pedagogical problems. It's an invitation that makes special sense at a time when so many faculty have twenty-plus years of experience to draw upon. In short, cases commend themselves because they honor and draw on the expertise that faculty have developed through experience.

> "I begin with the assumption that competent practitioners usually know more than they can say. They exhibit a kind of knowing-in-practice, most of which is tacit."
>
> *(Schön 1983, p. viii)*

Third, cases make teaching public. They do this first by recounting and describing episodes of teaching and learning. These episodes may or may not be blow-by-blow, verbatim accounts of actual events (as you will see in Chapter IV, on case writing, good case authors select and shape their material to make issues arise more suggestively). But whether cases are true in every detail or are realistic "composites," they open windows on practice that are all too rare on most campuses. They are also, importantly, *doors*, inviting others in to examine teaching and learning as a public event, to reflect out loud together about what works, and to raise issues of effectiveness and standards.

In all of these ways, cases have a special power to improve teaching — not so much by suggesting what to do in situation X, or how to do this or that on Monday morning (though certainly one can learn strategies and methods from cases). The distinctive contribution of cases is in promoting *a way of thinking about teaching*, one that recognizes teaching as a complex, intellectually engaging process of making decisions and solving problems in ambiguous situations. The use of cases is predicated on a view that the knowledge that effective teachers bring to their work (or need to be able to bring) is not simply a knowledge of methods, but one of substance and ideas — about one's field, about students, about learning, and about the complex relationships among these "variables" in real classrooms.

Cases, if you will, give teaching its due as an intellectual activity. In doing so, they speak not only to those "already converted" faculty who care about teaching (and show up for every teaching workshop) but also to those who have traditionally eschewed the topic — and without whom larger improvement cannot occur.

CHAPTER III

USING CASES ON YOUR CAMPUS
Three Examples, and Strategies for Making Them Work

Chapter II deals largely with the concept of the case — apart from its use — as a carrier of meaning, arguing that cases are a genre distinctly suited to capturing the kind of knowing that goes into teaching. But most case practitioners would agree with Harvard case writer Abby Hansen that, "Just as a piece of music exists only partially when it isn't being sung or played, a case comes fully to life only when it's being discussed" (in Christensen 1987, p. 265). Certainly, where the aim is to foster faculty conversation, the character of the discussion is as important as the case itself. But what does that discussion look like? How and where does it occur? How do you make one happen successfully?

This chapter answers those questions through three actual and quite different cases — which we hope you'll photocopy and try with colleagues on your campus. To help you do so, we've followed each case with suggestions for use — "teaching notes," as they're often called. These notes address issues that might be raised, alternative methods for discussion (such as the use of leaderless small groups), ideas about background and follow-up readings to enrich analysis, and ways to link the case with other teaching-improvement activities.

The aim here is to be concrete enough about the "how to" of using cases for you to make effective use of a case in your own setting, but sufficiently open-ended to encourage you to devise your *own* strategies for doing so. There is no single, right way of using cases. And although everyone gets better with practice (both facilitators and participants), there's nothing mysterious about case discussion, nothing "high tech." Indeed, one of the virtues of the genre is that cases work for so many people in such different settings, with such different styles. So, experiment. Trust your instincts as a teacher. And have a good time!

Case #1

This first case focuses on a kind of teaching that undergraduates on many campuses get in great doses: the large lecture. It was written by Clyde Herreid, distinguished teaching professor, Department of Biological Sciences, at SUNY Buffalo, who also, incidentally, uses cases with his students to teach an introductory biology course he recently developed as part of a new general-education program.

In the Beginning

by Clyde Freeman Herreid
Professor of Biology, SUNY Buffalo

Adam Henderson looked out at the three hundred faces listening to him expound on the Origin of Life. Here he was, halfway through the semester in General Biology and he was once again launched into a discussion of evolution. Adam realized he had students enthralled from his opening words read from the Bible, "In the beginning. . . ."

Adam was a distinguished teaching professor at State University, and this was one of his favorite lectures. Dressed in a dark conservative suit, reminiscent of a preacher in his Sunday best, he began with his reading of Genesis, Chapter I, which always immediately captivated the class and held them as he worked his way through each day's events in Creation Week.

The lecture's climax then brought him to his personal version of Genesis, which he read to a background of choral music. . . . "In the beginning there was hydrogen . . ." and ending with, "it was neither good, nor was it bad, it merely was." This always brought a great round of applause at the close of lecture, and Adam looked forward to the response that had sustained him for thirty years of teaching.

Today's class was going just as planned, Adam thought as he finished his opening reading of Genesis and went smoothly on to mention other versions of the origin of life according to various religions and mythologies. All of this was a prelude for the scientific views he wished to discuss that day. This lecture was a show stopper, moving from the striking introduction through the modern observations of astronomers, geologists, and chemists showing how the first living things could have originated out of organic soup formed on primitive Earth.

Adam finished with his general introduction and turned on the overhead projector. He spoke of the early days of the universe as described in the now famous Big Bang model. The first few moments of the universe led to the production of hydrogen, then helium. All other elements were to come much later, forged in the solar furnaces of the stars, he told students. He spoke of the formation of the galaxies and star systems in the expanding universe and about how our own sun and solar system were formed ten billion years after the Big Bang and had been in existence less than five billion years.

Adam flipped on another overhead and began to explain the astronomers' views on the interaction of gravitation, which pulled matter together into a forming solar system, while angular momentum tended to throw matter back into space. As he spoke of the impact that gravity must have had on the formation of the early days of the sun and its planets, Adam suddenly heard a voice speak loudly, "Gravity is only a theory."

Adam glanced to the middle of the class, looking for the speaker. There she was, a round-faced young woman with an intense look on her face. Adam recognized her from previous brief conversations he had had with her after class. She always seemed to ask questions that were slightly unusual, off-center from the topic, speaking with a clipped staccato voice and with little expression. Here she was blurting out abruptly in the midst of his carefully crafted lecture.

Adam was puzzled; did he hear her correctly? "What?" he asked in a slightly irritated voice. He had a finely timed lecture to give, yet he wished to be reasonable. Any serious deviations would mean he could not cover the critical experiments of Miller and Urey or Fox, and he certainly would not reach the climax of the lecture, to read a scientist's version of Genesis, which put the whole problem in perspective.

"What did you say?" he repeated. The lecture hall was suddenly deadly silent.

"Gravity is only a theory." ■

Teaching Notes and Suggestions for Using "In the Beginning"

If you're thinking of trying cases on your campus, "In the Beginning" might be a good one to start with. It's lively and short; it focuses on the sciences, where talk about teaching is often scant; and it raises a number of salient issues for faculty in almost any discipline.

A first, right-on-the-surface issue raised by the case has to do with the lecture method, the virtues and limits of which are seen here in full relief. Discussion might focus on the appropriateness of the lecture method to the setting and subject matter; it might focus on problems posed by the method and how Adam handles those problems. Are there, participants might ask themselves, other strategies he might have used with a class of this size? What are the alternatives? Are there ways to cover material (as Adam is bent on doing) and involve students at the same time?

Relatedly, the case raises the issue of role: Adam is clearly the authority, delivering up his expertise; his students are expected to learn what he already knows and, presumably, to be infected with his enthusiasm along the way. How appropriate are these roles? Is there anything to be said about the implied model of teaching as performance — complete with the anticipation of applause from students? (The comment in the box *right* by English professor Jane Tompkins, of Duke University, may provide a suggestive context for discussion.)

> **Teacher as Performer**
>
> "I had always thought that what I was doing was helping my students to understand the material we were studying.... What I was actually concerned with and focused on most of the time were three things: (a) to show the students how smart I was, (b) to show them how knowledgeable I was, and (c) to show them how well-prepared I was for class....
>
> How did it come to be that our main goal as academics turned out to be performance? I think the answer to the question is fairly complicated, but here is one way to go. Each person comes into a professional situation dragging along behind her a long bag full of desires, fears, expectations, needs, resentments — the list goes on. But the main component is fear. Fear is the driving force behind the performance model.... I became aware recently that my own fear of being shown up for what I really am must transmit itself to my students, and insofar as I was afraid to be exposed, they too would be afraid."
>
> *(Tompkins 1990, p. 654)*

Most obviously, perhaps, the case begs for discussion of the student's comment, "Gravity is only a theory." How should Adam respond to her? What are the options? The risks and opportunities? Of course, the answers here depend (as they do in the heat of the classroom moment) on what one makes of the student's comment. Is her comment a red herring, or a mark of more subtle understanding? She is, after all, correct in a certain sense, and the case sets the stage for discussion of how we help students understand distinctions among *theory, hypothesis, fact,* and *paradigm*. Of course, the student's comment also invites discussion about religious belief (a possible explanation for her comment) in the science classroom. And what, for that matter, are we to make of *Adam's* use of religion: Is his reading and paraphrase of the Bible and choral music at the end of the lecture appropriate? Offensive? Effective? What factors should influence our answers to these questions?

Exactly which of the above lines of discussion are pursued depends of course on the interests and concerns of participants. And it's worth thinking about how — and how well — the case will "play" with different groups. The chair of the biology department might want to bring this case to a departmental retreat to encourage discussion of alternatives to the lecture method. Alternatively, the case might be just the thing for an all-faculty workshop on teaching large classes sponsored by the campus teaching and learning center. It's short enough, too, for the sort of no-agenda, brown-bag lunch sessions that faculty organize on many campuses to discuss their teaching.

One final point: "In the Beginning" may well raise issues that aren't even hinted at above; there's a bit of the Rorschach in most cases, and that's part of the virtue of the case method. So think in advance about issues that seem likely to arise, and make an outline/discussion plan, as suggested by Rita Silverman and William Welty in the box on page 30, but be prepared to let the discussion take its own course, as well.

Case #2

The second case is one of a growing set being developed at the Pace University Center for Case Studies in Education, with funding from FIPSE, to explore issues of diversity in the classroom. The authors, both from Pace, are William Welty, professor of management and director of faculty development, and Rita Silverman, professor of teacher education.

Grant Eldridge

*by
William Welty
Professor of Management and
Director of Faculty Development
and
Rita Silverman
Professor of Teacher Education
Pace University*

"It's a goddam United Nations in there," Grant Eldridge, professor of sociology at Metropolitan University, fumed to Anna Johnston, his closest friend in the department. Anna waved Grant to the chair next to her desk, but Grant shook his head and remained facing Anna, leaning toward her with his hands spread palms down on her desk.

"Anything I can do, Grant?" Anna asked.

"Well, for starters, you could help me get some release time. If I'm going to have classes filled with students who don't speak the language, who can't read the textbook, and who can't write decent papers, I'll need a cut in my teaching load so I'll have time to tutor some of them and to read and respond to their work."

"Be serious, Grant. If you got release time, everyone in the department would be demanding release time. You know that. What is it you really want?"

Grant finally took the chair Anna had offered earlier and admitted, "I don't know what I want. Better students, I guess. I've been here for more than twenty years and for the past five the quality of students has deteriorated rapidly. Teaching them is like pulling teeth. They cut classes regularly and don't bother to call or to have excuses. They have no interest in sociology, they don't want to learn new things, they have no interest in ideas, they don't want to put in the time to study. . . ." He paused, stopping himself in mid-complaint. When Anna didn't say anything, he went on, "It's more than their attitudes though. The worst part is that they're dumb. They can't read, they can't write, they can't think." As he finished, Grant realized he was almost shouting. "I'm sorry, Anna. I know it's not your fault — you just had the bad luck to be sitting in your office on a day when I'm particularly frustrated."

Anna smiled. "Tell me why you're so frustrated now," she said.

"Why now? That's easy. I've just left the worst of four bad classes I've been assigned to teach this semester."

"What's so bad about this group, particularly?"

"Really, the question should be, 'What's so bad about your classes generally?'" Grant's voice rose as he again started to tell Anna that the students were not interested in learning, that their skills were weak, and so on.

Anna interrupted him. "Grant, it would help me if you could be specific. Tell me about the class you just left."

"Okay. It's an Intro to Sociology class — thirty-seven students. Most are freshmen and sophomores, but a few are upperclassmen, maybe six or seven. Let me find the class list I created — at least half of them have names I can't pronounce."

Grant began digging in his briefcase. As he looked, he went on, "The first day of class I asked them to fill out an information sheet. I do that to get some background on the kids, but also to see if they can write in full sentences, how they use the language, things like that. I used to ask questions like 'What books have had the greatest influence on you?' or 'What social issues are you interested in?' but now I ask 'What language is spoken in your home?' and 'In what country were you born? Your parents?'"

Anna nodded. "And? What did you find?"

"First of all, I found that too many of them can't write a simple sentence. And their parents don't speak English. A lot of them weren't born here. They come from Colombia, or Bolivia, or countries like that. And there are about twelve black students — some from the area, but some who come from Haiti, Uganda, you know."

"So you have a diverse population?"

"Anna, look at this list."

Anna took the sheet of paper Grant had pulled from his briefcase. "What do the asterisks mean?"

"Those are the black students."

"How did you get the SATs and averages?"

"I had the secretary pull their SATs and grade-point averages off the computer. That's how I found out that most of these kids lack the ability to meet my requirements."

"What are your requirements for this class?"

"Just what you'd expect, Anna. They have to do a research paper on a topic of their choice; I give quizzes, a mid-term, and a final, based on the readings and the lectures. . . ."

Anna interrupted to ask, "What kinds of questions?"

"The quizzes are usually short answer — a couple of words or a sentence at the most. I just gave the mid-term. They had fifty multiple-choice items worth one point each and eight short essays — they had to answer five."

"What kinds of items?" Anna asked again.

"I took them directly from the test bank in the Instructor's Manual. I used to try to create questions of my own, but I got so much flak about ambiguous questions that now I copy them word for word from the questions in the Manual, and if students argue, I refer them to the page in the book that the question was taken from — the Manual provides that information. I've been thinking of putting the page number by the question, so that the ones who are interested can go directly to the source for the questions they got wrong."

"And how did you grade them?"

"Fifty percent for the multiple choice; each essay was worth ten points, and I gave partial credit. They had two hours to complete the exam."

SOCIOLOGY 100 — SPRING, 1991

NAME	SEX	BORN	GPA	SAT
Abramowitz, Ruth	F	Israel	2.9	830
Bakasuldis, Tina	F	USA	3.6	1190
Banacoda, Edwina	F	Colombia	2.8	970
Catalenda, Christine	F	Philippines	2.0	N/A
Casten, Thomas*	M	USA	2.2	960
Charles, June	F	USA	3.4	790
Cotten, Alan	M	USA	2.3	830
Dasheau, Illia*	F	Haiti	2.0	1000
DeLong, Robert	M	USA	2.8	770
Esler, Anthony	M	USA	1.2	1190
Ferinala, Emuradu*	M	Nigeria	2.1	N/A
Goodward, Richard	M	USA	2.8	920
Gagliandio, Mary	F	USA	2.2	610
Henry, Kim*	F	USA	3.3	1060
Hopkins, Kareem*	M	USA	2.3	930
Ilo, David	M	Philippines	2.8	740
Jasten, Derwi	M	St. Croix	2.6	900
Lasser, Paul	M	USA	2.4	880
Moore, Keri*	F	USA	3.1	700
Martinez, Lulu	F	Dom. Republic	2.7	820
Mascola, Arthur	M	USA	4.0	1250
Napoli, Michael	M	USA	2.7	900
Nadpuda, Ranni	F	Iran	3.5	N/A
Oliva, Rosabelle	F	Puerto Rico	1.7	800
Panaletta, Marie	F	Yugoslavia	2.3	770
Polaccio, Francis	M	USA	2.7	1000
Reed, Afreeka*	F	USA	1.0	720
Rosasario, Violet	F	Dom. Republic	1.9	900
Sadharta, Sangeeth	F	India	3.7	850
Schlatter, Alice	F	Scotland	3.3	850
Smith, Washington*	M	USA	2.7	1070
Silver, Karen	F	USA	2.4	900
Viggario, Maria	F	USA	3.7	1070
Varden, Annette*	F	USA	1.9	900
Westlake, Peter	M	USA	2.9	1060
Zivic, John	M	Yugoslavia	0.3	N/A
Zoarand, Ally	F	USA	3.3	900

"And how did they do?" Anna looked interested.

"The scores ranged from 31 to 94 — the median was 63. I'd have to check for sure, but I think there were only two scores in the 90s, half a dozen in the 80s, maybe eight in the 70s. More than half the class got Ds or Fs."

"How did the students respond to the grades?"

"Anger from some, but mostly lack of interest. I could have been talking about the weather for all the response I got from them. That was today's class, which probably explains why I'm so disgusted. After I went over their tests and realized how poorly most of them did, I thought I'd give them a second chance to learn the material by debriefing the test. So, I took what I consider to be valuable class time to go over the items, one by one, and to discuss the essay questions. What a waste of time — I couldn't get anyone to talk, to ask questions, anything. You'd think they'd all gotten perfect papers for the interest they showed. What's clear is that they don't care to learn anything; they just want to get through the class as painlessly as possible. Sociology means nothing to them, and they don't want it to. I'll bet they're in that particular section of sociology because it fulfills a core requirement and they needed an 11:00 class on Tuesdays and Thursdays."

As Grant finished speaking, Anna was laughing aloud. "I know, I know," she said. "When I asked my Monday night economics class why they were there, more than half of the students said that economics was a required course in their program and they were closed out of a day section."

Grant could not bring himself to smile at Anna's comment. Tartly, he said, "I don't know why you think that's funny — that's my point exactly, and it's one of the things that's wrong with these students." He sighed and stood up, preparing to leave Anna's office. "I've lost my sense of humor, I guess. Nothing about this place is funny to me anymore."

Anna looked contrite. "I wasn't making fun of you, Grant. I was sympathizing, really. It just strikes me as funny that they admit why they're in a particular section. I'm not sure we were any different — we just never would have told a professor the truth. These students will. Maybe we should admire their candor."

Anna's comments did not improve Grant's mood. "You can call it candor — I think it's stupidity. They don't know enough to say the right thing. I don't think they even hear how offensive that kind of response is, which confirms for me that they aren't smart enough to be in college. What on earth are they going to be like when they're out of here and working full-time?"

Anna stood up and walked with Grant toward his office. "Is there anything I can do? Would it help if I sat in on a class?"

Grant smiled for the first time that day as he walked alongside his friend. Then he nodded. "I hate to burden you, but maybe if you saw the class in action, you could give me some advice. Can you come on Thursday? The class meets from 11:00 to 11:50 in Spruce Hall, Room 311."

Anna nodded. I'll see you then," she said as she turned back to her office.

* * *

Two days later, Anna slid into an empty tablet-arm desk at the end of a row in Room 311 just as Grant was taking attendance. When he saw her, he stopped, introduced her to the group, and handed her a seating chart and a copy of his class list. Anna smiled as students turned to look at her. Some of the students smiled back. She recognized several students from her own classes or from her freshman advising sessions. The classroom was large and bright. There were six rows of eight desks each, and the thirty-two students present that day were sitting toward the back of the room. The front two or three desks in each row were empty.

Grant began the class by reminding the students that their term papers were due in two weeks and asking if the students had any questions about the assignment. A young woman sitting two seats in front of Anna raised her hand.

Grant consulted his seating chart and said, "Yes, Violet. What's your question?"

Without looking directly at Grant, Violet asked, "How many references do we have to use?"

Grant looked exasperated. "I'm not going to say, because then everyone will take the minimum number and stop when you have that many. That's not how you do research for a term paper. You should seek out as many references as you can, take notes on them, and then, as you write your paper, include the ones that support your points. If I give you a minimum number, say five, you'll all find five references and then start writing your paper without having really dug into the topic. Let me tell you that two or three is too few, and twenty-five is probably too many. You need to figure out the right number depending on your topic and how hard you are willing to work. Okay, Violet?"

Violet didn't respond to Grant's question, and Grant did not repeat it. "Any other questions about the term paper?" Another hand went up. Grant again consulted the seating chart. "Thomas, what's your question?"

The student answered, "I'm Anthony. Tom sits behind me. Do the papers have to be typed?"

This time, Grant could not hide his annoyance. "Of course the papers have to be typed. Didn't you read the assignment? Does anyone have any questions about the *content* of the term papers?"

When no one responded, Grant began the lecture. "As we begin Chapter 10, 'The Evolution of Clans in European Society,' it's important to think about the key points from Chapter 9."

As soon as Grant began to speak, students opened their notebooks and picked up their pens. Grant, noticing the flurry of activity, said, "You don't have to write this down. It's in the book at the end of Chapter 9, in the summary section. I just wanted you to see how the material we've been studying relates to the material we are about to study."

Despite his words, most of the students tried to write down everything he was saying. Grant spoke for several minutes about the earliest clans — how their activities evolved from simple groups, who banded together informally for protection, into more complex structures, made up of diverse members, and how these groups began to develop into formal organizations. Anna knew that over the years, Grant had gathered many examples and stories to use in an introductory sociology course. While the department switched to a more current text every two or three years, the topics in an introductory course remained fairly consistent, so his store of examples served him well as he developed lectures to supplement the readings the students were required to do. In the more than twenty years that he had been teaching, he had acquired a reputation as an interesting lecturer, one who could command the students' attention with both his presence and his presentation. Anna realized that the skill had not deserted him; she became very interested in his lecture.

After several minutes, Grant paused and asked, "Who remembers how the book described the first clans?" No hands went up. Grant consulted his seating chart and said, "June?"

June gazed down at her hands, resting on her notebook. Without lifting her eyes, she responded, "They were informal?"

Grant glanced at Anna and then gently said to June, "Are you asking or telling, June?"

The student didn't respond, so Grant said, "Yes, the first clans were informal. What else do you know about them? Sangeeth?"

Sangeeth consulted her notes and read back much of what Grant had said in his earlier remarks. Grant nodded as she spoke and said, when she had paused, "Good work, Sangeeth. Now, could you put that into your own words?"

The student looked at Grant with a serious expression and replied, "No, sir."

Again, Grant looked at Anna, who did not return his gaze.

Grant asked, "Would anyone like to say, in your own words, what you know about clans?" There was no response. Several students were slumping down in their chairs, looking as if they were trying to disappear in case Grant decided to consult his seating chart again. Instead, Grant chose to end the torture by continuing his lecture. As soon as he began to speak, some of the slumping students again sat up and started to write.

Grant spoke for about twenty more minutes, going to the board to write down key words, returning to the lectern to consult his notes, pacing in front of the class. Many of the students followed his movements, and no one fell asleep. Occasionally, students would turn around to glance at Anna in the back of the room.

With ten minutes left in the period, Grant began peppering the class with questions. He called on students using the seating chart. While he did not seem to have an obvious pattern for his questions, it was clear to Anna that he was jumping around the room, moving from front to back, from side to side. The questions appeared to be written into his lecture notes, and he marked off each question as he asked it. When he did not get the answer he wanted, or if an answer was not complete, he would answer the question himself, reminding the students that these were the kinds of questions that would be on the final and that if they had done the reading prior to today's class, they would be able to answer these questions and that the lecture would have had more meaning. While the answers, on the few occasions when he got answers at all, were not very good, the students wrote down the questions. They treated everything he said, even discussion questions, as fodder for their incessant note taking.

At 11:47 by Anna's watch, the students began to do what she called the end-of-period dance. By 11:49, every notebook was closed, pens were put away, other materials were gathered, coats were on. Faculty could teach classes without a watch — the students would signal when time was up.

Grant answered his final questions, reminded them of the reading for the next class, and dismissed the class, saying, "Have a good weekend. Try to work on your term papers between movies and parties."

The students filed out noisily. A couple said, "Have a nice weekend, Dr. Eldridge," but most chatted with each other, ignoring him. Grant erased the chalkboard, gathered up his materials, and waited for Anna to join him at the front of the room. They left in silence, unable to speak because of the noise as students erupted from classrooms along the corridor.

Once outside the building, he turned to Anna and asked, "So, dear friend, what advice do you have for me?" ∎

Teaching Notes and Suggestions for Using "Grant Eldridge"

Rich with data, full of moments and details that lend themselves to group analysis and problem solving, "Grant Eldridge" almost ensures a lively discussion. The authors suggest two rather different ways to take advantage of the case's potential, depending on your objectives and on time constraints.

A fairly traditional approach would be to begin the case discussion with a question about Grant's dilemma: "Grant Eldridge has asked for help in his teaching. How do you think he would describe his problems?" After a discussion of how Grant sees the problems, the discussion leader can complicate the analysis by asking participants for their *own* account of Grant's teaching. This question, which may emerge naturally from the discussion that follows the first question, will most likely provoke an avalanche of responses from the group. In fact, the leader's task may be to prevent the discussion from becoming a "Let's dump on Grant!" session, since the central character in the case must remain a real person, not some stick figure who represents all bad teaching, if the "lessons" of the case are to be personally felt by participants.

> ### Prediscussion Planning
> "We suggest that there are four elements of prediscussion planning for the case discussion leader — determining the *teaching/learning objectives*; understanding the *blocks of discussion* — the issues the case raises — and deciding which of these blocks she/he wishes to emphasize; planning a *question outline* — a set of questions that will encourage discussion of key issues and that will lead to achieving the teaching objectives; and planning a *board outline* — a plan for what the chalkboard or flip charts might look like at the end of the discussion."
> *(Silverman and Welty 1992, p. 269)*

By the end of these first two segments of discussion, the chalkboard can be a powerful aid to further analysis, listing problems from Grant's perspective and from the discussion group's perspective. Note that in describing these problems, the participants also will be relating the facts of the case — descriptions of the students, the physical setup of the room, Grant's teaching behaviors, his interactions with students. These facts also can be recorded on the board so that, at the end of this first phase of the discussion, the board will be a sort of map of what seems most important to the discussion group — which may or may not jibe with issues the discussion leader had in mind, but are the source of this method's power. Indeed, one of the important balancing acts case discussion leaders must perform is to stay focused on the case at hand (not allowing "war stories" and weird tangents), while at the same time allowing the discussion to reflect the real concerns of the participants.

Once the facts and problems of the case have been identified and analyzed, the discussion can turn to the question of action. "Grant has asked for help. Let's play the role of Anna here. What would you say to Grant about his teaching? What advice would you give him?" If the earlier discussion has focused on both naming and analyzing the problems, this part of the discussion can be minimized and really will turn on a consideration of how much bad news Grant can bear. The discussion leader might choose to record the responses by categorizing them into a range of solutions, from some small, immediate changes in Grant's teaching, all the way to completely changing his course design for next semester. However, if the discussion is limited to an hour or so, there clearly will not be time enough to fully explore the solution phase.

If a longer block of time is available, an alternative approach might be considered in order to focus more extensively on solutions, using the case as a kind of "centerpiece" around which a set of activities unfolds over time. This approach begins by coupling the case with background readings to give faculty a shared conceptual framework for case discussion. A first reading that Silverman and Welty have used to good effect is "Skewered on the Unicorn's Horn: The Illusion of Tragic Tradeoff Between Content and Critical Thinking in the Teaching of Science," by Craig Nelson.[1] Nelson's piece is useful, Silverman says, in acquainting faculty with William Perry's work and in raising issues about "where the students in the case are as thinkers." A second piece by J. D. Bransford[2] suggests that when students are unsuccessful, it is often a case of mismatch — between what *students* bring to their learning (what they know and how they prepare) and what *teachers* bring to their teaching in the form of methods, requirements, and materials. Other, roughly parallel readings obviously could substitute for these two, Silverman says, but these work well in framing and informing the discussion of what is, after all, a complicated and controversial case.

Such readings also provide a bridge to activities that might follow the discussion of "Grant Eldridge." "What we've asked people to do," Silverman says, "is to take Bransford's concept of match and mismatch, which the group has already applied to the case, and to go back and apply it to their own teaching." Following the case discussion session, each participant identifies a problem in a class he or she teaches, diagnoses it in terms of the concepts dealt with in discussing "Grant Eldridge," and devises appropriate strategies for solving the problem. This "assignment" is then the basis for a follow-up session, in which the "cases" in question now are faculty's own, from their own classes, which is, after all, "what we're ultimately after, . . . for faculty to be as reflective about their own practice as they are in formal case discussion sessions," Silverman says.

---

[1] *Enhancing Critical Thinking in the Sciences*, edited by Linda W. Crow, (Washington, D.C.: Society for College Science Teachers, an affiliate of the National Science Teachers Association, 1989).

[2] *Human Cognition: Learning, Understanding, and Remembering*, (Belmont, Calif.: Wadsworth, 1979).

Case #3

The third case describes the first day of a course in which students will be working to improve their abilities as writers. Of particular note is the inclusion in the case of data from students — *actual* responses from *actual* students in a course like the one featured in the case. Indeed, the case is as much about students as about the teacher, who (in contrast to Grant Eldridge of Case #2) remains almost wholly anonymous. The case was written by Deanna Yameen, instructor and critical-thinking specialist, and Elizabeth Fideler, associate dean for teaching/learning and professional development, Massachusetts Bay Community College (Fideler has since taken a position at Recruiting New Teachers, Inc., in Belmont, Massachusetts).

See You On Wednesday!

*by
Deanna Yameen
Instructor and Critical-Thinking Specialist
Massachusetts Bay Community College
and
Elizabeth Fideler
Recruiting New Teachers, Inc.*

The first class meeting seemed to go smoothly enough. I went in, introduced myself, and ran through the course syllabus and calendar. The students seemed pretty much like the students I taught at State U. — maybe a little older. They asked the same questions about how long the papers should be and which books to buy. They made no comments about the journal assignment for the next class. They filled out my survey readily enough. In fact, class ended twenty minutes early.

In my eight years of teaching at State U., I never saw anything like the survey responses I received from this class. Can community college students be *that* different? I just don't know how I'm going to cope.

I used the same survey I used at State U., with exactly the same directions: "I'm just looking for some information to get a feel for the class. Tell me (1) why you are taking the class, and (2) what you want me to know about you. Please be honest. You don't have to sign your name if you'd rather not."

Then I read their responses. What have I gotten myself into? What am I going to do on Wednesday?

Take a look at the responses for yourself:

```
Learn to write very, very well

I want you to know is that the main reason for me to
learn, is because I wanna go to computer afterwards.

This is my first class in college. Since I graduated I
wanted to try writing to see if I didn't have the ability.

I am a international student. Sometimes I don't speak or
tell what I want to say well.

I want to how to use research information then write
paper.


To enter nursing program, and have a good abilities.
```

You should know that I have a learning disable.

I have a Learning Disability in Reading and I think my writing is Poor.

I would like to prove to myself that I am am now ready to be a serious student and that I can get an A in this class.

I failed out of school and it has taken me a long time to get the guts to try again. I really want to do well.

I have taken this course last semester and wrote three essay.

A lot of things come very easily to me but what does not I become easily frustrated which makes it that much harder. I have to read lips. I am slightly tone deaf.

I would like to learn how to get my thoughts down in an organized fashion. I would like my writing to be impressive and express how I feel.

I would like to write a paper on my own that really makes sense.

I want to be able to write a good essay, or other papers I might have to write in my college days.

I want to be prepared for the other courses for my college education. I want to improve my writing skills.

I'd like read different kinds of books and I want to try to like writing.

I want to learn to read and think about a situation or article and know what to write about.

Teaching Notes and Suggestions for Using "See You On Wednesday!"

This case, the authors say, was conceived in response to the reality that students today are increasingly diverse in their backgrounds and expectations, a point vividly made by the student comments contained in the case (which you might replace with comments from students on your own campus if you want to tie the case more directly to your own setting). An obvious point of departure for discussion of the case is people's responses to those student comments. What do we make of them? What items stand out? What range of student goals and expectations are evident? Is this kind of diversity a *problem*, or might it be an *opportunity* for learning? How do you handle such diversity in your own classes? What — most pointedly — does one *do* "on Wednesday," given what students say about their expectations?

"See You On Wednesday!" not only raises issues about the diversity of classrooms today; it also illustrates the need for faculty to find out more about their students as learners. "First and foremost," say Fideler and Yameen, "we wanted to stimulate inquiry into teaching and learning issues." Indeed, the case models a Classroom Assessment strategy for engaging in such inquiry. Another line of discussion, then, might focus on the usefulness of the strategy employed in the case, and suggestions for alternative or additional strategies.

An additional set of issues the case raises for some faculty, the authors have found, is "a sort of philosophical one." What faculty see as they read through the list of student comments depends in good part on their philosophy of the teaching of writing (and perhaps of teaching more generally). Does one focus, for instance, on the problems of punctuation? How important *are* the mechanics of writing? What about writing as a means of self-expression, as a process of discovery and learning? During the case discussion, these questions, the authors say, can raise the decibel level among faculty participants (of whatever discipline) who see themselves as having responsibility for student writing; the questions lead as well into larger issues about "standards" and about who ought to be in college. . . .

"See You On Wednesday!" was originally intended for use with "new hires" at Massachusetts Bay Community College, who might have had teaching experience but not necessarily in a community college. However, the case also has been used successfully with experienced community college faculty and with a group of faculty developers. With all of these audiences, the authors had good luck with a small-group discussion method. Directions to the groups were short and simple:

- Have group members introduce themselves.
- Read the case.
- Describe the class portrayed in the case.
- Consider these questions, given the student population in the class:
  — What kinds of in-class activities or homework assignments would you suggest to the instructor?
  — What would *you* do on Wednesday?
- Suggest how the teacher in the case could continue to gather information beyond this first class session about how the students are learning.

Following small-group discussions, a debriefing of the entire group gives people a chance to hear from other groups and to generate a still wider range of strategies.

Like "Grant Eldridge," "See You On Wednesday!" might be enhanced by appropriate framing materials: an article on Classroom Research, a piece on teaching adult students, a good summary (perhaps by a member of the English department) of different schools of thought about the teaching of writing. Such materials could be read in advance of the case discussion to give participants a more conceptual frame of reference for their responses; alternatively, the case discussion could be followed up with such materials as a segue to subsequent activities.

Another possibility: Following a discussion of the case, several faculty might be asked to write up their answer to the "What to do on Wednesday?" question, then bring their ideas back to the group for a second-stage discussion.

Tips for Case Discussion Leaders

In addition to the suggestions for use appended to each of the cases in this chapter, you may find the following six tips for case discussion leaders helpful.

1. Think hard about the setting. A good case discussion can't happen unless people can see and hear one another. If you've got the right kind of space, a large group will work (Harvard Business School case classrooms are tiered to "minimize physical distance and to maximize psychological togetherness"; they hold up to eighty people). But groups of thirty or forty may be more practical in most settings. Some case practitioners claim that with fewer than that there's insufficient difference of opinion, and it's harder to keep the energy level high. Others are using small groups (six to eight people) with success (see Teaching Notes for "See You On Wednesday!" in this chapter).

2. If people don't know one another, large nametags, readable from across the room, make it possible to call participants by name — a good idea not only to personalize the discussion but to help the leader direct the discussion.

3. Most case facilitators want a board, easel, or overhead to help organize the discussion and give it shape. A trick of the trade is to know what you want the board to look like at the end of the session even before the discussion begins.

4. Have a plan for starting the discussion. There's nothing so disconcerting as to lob out a first question and have nothing come back. You may want to decide in advance whom you want to call on. You may want to give people two minutes of "free-writing" time to ensure that everyone has something they can lob back. You may want to let people begin with three-minute buzz sessions with their neighbor. . . . What you don't want is to begin on a flustered, uncertain note.

5. Have a plan for closing the discussion. There's disagreement about the degree of closure that's appropriate to cases. Some practitioners insist that the purpose of the case method is to instill a kind of thinking that makes closure inappropriate, but the fact is that most audiences want some sense of an ending. And, of course, an ending need not mean "the answer." One might, for instance, ask three or four people from the audience to make a final comment on the discussion. The final five minutes might be used for the group to brainstorm insights and lessons from the case, which could be recorded on the blackboard then later typed up and distributed. The discussion might turn a corner at the end, from a focus on the case itself to comments about "neat ideas" from the discussion or questions that arose that might be grist for a future discussion.

6. Study the work of other case discussion leaders. Styles vary enormously, from the contentious to the counseling and therapeutic. Find one that matches you and your purposes..

CHAPTER IV

CASE WRITING ON YOUR CAMPUS

A number of campuses where faculty began by *discussing* cases rather quickly turned to case writing — and with good reason. The process of *writing* cases encourages faculty to step back from their own teaching and reflect upon it; it forces processes of inquiry that otherwise might not occur. As a faculty member who set out to write a case about her educational psychology course told me, "Suddenly I was asking new questions about what was going on in students' heads; I found I couldn't teach the course the same way." Along the way, case writing also promotes collaboration and communication about what goes on in the classroom, opening the classroom door, uncovering the scholarly aspects of teaching. This chapter reports on these and other benefits of case writing by recounting how two different faculty groups undertook to develop cases about teaching and learning in their own settings.

The Washington Center for Improving the Quality of Undergraduate Education

In 1991, a dozen faculty in the state of Washington began work on a set of cases designed to "arouse curiosity about collaborative education, stimulate new teaching teams and programs, encourage conversations among administrators . . . and put many groups to work designing solutions to intriguing instructional, interpersonal, and administrative challenges" (Washington Center "Casebook," p. 1). The product of their work, a set of cases, with a thoughtful preface on their use, is now available from the Washington Center (see Resources in the Appendix for more.)

The history of the "Casebook" goes back a number of years. Since its inception in 1985, the Washington Center for Improving the Quality of Undergraduate Education, an interinstitutional consortium focused on "low-cost, high-yield" approaches to educational reform, has had a committee on evaluation. Over the years, the committee's work has included a number of efforts to study and increase the effects of collaborative learning and learning communities on students, faculty, and institutional change. Several years ago, when the state's mandate for assessment was rolled into place, some of that work was taken up by individual campuses, and the Center stepped back to reconsider its evaluation agenda. What turned up at the top of its new list were issues of improving and sustaining collaborative teaching and learning, and it was with such a need in mind that a subcommittee of the evaluation committee decided to give cases — cases were, as one participant put it, "in the air" — a try.

An early, key event in that effort was the experience of a case. The twelve-person subcommittee devoted an afternoon's discussion to "The Case of the Dethroned Section Leader," one of the cases in C. Roland Christensen's *Teaching and the Case Method* (1987). Until then, reports Barbara Leigh Smith, the group's coordinator, "Most of us just didn't really get it. We weren't quite sure what a case *was*. The experience of a case and case discussion persuaded us that the method worked and that we could use it."

A next step was to decide on topics. What should the group write cases *about*? On the one hand, this question was answered by beginning with "people's passions," Smith says; it was felt that the best cases would be the ones about issues people cared about and really wanted to explore. On the other hand, it was possible to sort out options and choose among them on the basis of issues identified over the previous several years in interviews with campuses that were using the learning community model. The interviews suggested that the problems posed by collaborative learning required cases not only about pedagogical concerns but also about faculty teamwork, administrative support, and institutional change.

Much of the most important work of the group occurred during three 2-day retreats. With their latest drafts in hand, group members gathered to read cases aloud and talk . . . and talk some more about where each case needed more information, flesh put on bones, sharper focus, or missing voices written in. As cases went through this process, they became increasingly collaborative products — so much so that the group elected not to name individual authors, a decision that also spoke to concerns about confidentiality and sensitivity on individual campuses.

Along the way, there were some nice surprises. "We thought the creative writers in the bunch would lead the way," says Smith. "But our cases came from faculty with all sorts of different backgrounds. Lots of people turned out to be reflective in ways that we really hadn't known before."

Next steps in the Washington Center's work with cases focus on their use to promote change and improvement. The group plans to continue to write new cases and to refine the ones they have already developed by using them on a pilot basis in workshops and retreats. Case facilitators were trained, several campuses identified as sites for case discussion, and plans put in place to use cases for new faculty training and in a retreat for administrators. An added benefit, the case writers say, is that a number of their cases will probably turn up in classrooms, as well, for use with students; cases such as "Whose Agenda?" (in Additional Cases in the Appendix) can move students toward a greater awareness of their own role in the learning process.

It will be some time before all the effects of the Washington Center's work on cases can be assessed. But for those involved, the process already has brought considerable benefits. Smith notes, "The key for us has been working interinstitutionally. Some issues are too hard to talk about locally; sensitivity runs too high. Writing cases collaboratively across campuses allowed us to air issues that would have been impossible otherwise." And cases have been an important vehicle for perspective-taking, she adds. "Our case group involves faculty from such diverse institutions and disciplines . . . we're learning so much from each other!"

Florida Community College at Jacksonville (FCCJ)

It was at a national conference on teaching and learning that two FCCJ faculty first heard about AAHE's project to develop cases about college teaching and learning. Intrigued by the prospect of developing such cases on their own campus, Susan Hill and Betsy Griffey met with colleagues on the steering committee for FCCJ's Center for the Advancement of Teaching and Learning and set the date for a workshop to explore the idea. Eight months later, they had a set of nine faculty-authored cases, which have since been discussed in faculty-development settings on campus and beyond.

The first workshop, in September 1991, was attended by twenty faculty who had some preliminary interest in cases; its major outcome was to reinforce that interest, as audience members had an opportunity to engage in a case discussion and to begin brainstorming cases of their own. It was, however, after this brief foray into cases that the real work began.

It began a mere three weeks later, with the first of several case-writing workshops, facilitated by faculty affiliated with the Center. This initial workshop expanded the circle of faculty participants and continued earlier brainstorming for issues and situations that would make for good cases. Two months later, when the group gathered for a day-long session, they were able to identify characteristics of effective cases and a checklist of case-writing guidelines (see box). Most important, they worked in pairs to outline and actually write drafts of cases. Those drafts were then the focus of a final work session at the end of January 1992, focusing on revision. Drafts were circulated in advance and participants came with ideas, responses, and suggestions about one another's work.

FCCJ's Tips for Case Writing
- Limit the scope.
- Focus on conflict between goals and actuality.
- Base the case on an actual occurrence.
- Include an element of hope.
- Be specific.
- Include characters who are motivated to improve.
- Raise questions.
- Experiment with form (use drama, dialogue, etc.).
- Consider cases focused on students.

Final drafts were completed in March 1992, and the entire set now has been collected, printed, and distributed to interested faculty within the institution and to "friends of the project" elsewhere. (See Resources in the Appendix for information on ordering a free copy.)

Notably, Jacksonville faculty, like faculty at the Washington Center, proceeded largely on the basis of their own good sense and evolving experience. "We had our moments of doubt," says one of the participants, "wondering if what we were doing was going to work, whether our cases were any good. But one of the benefits of working as a group was to talk each other through those moments."

Plans are now under way to introduce cases into various ongoing campus activities: Case discussions are on tap for "Campus Spotlight" sessions, where faculty gather to talk about teaching; *Centerline*, the newsletter of the Center for the Advancement of Teaching and Learning, will feature cases; and cases will be used in workshops for adjunct faculty.

But the value of the case-writing work in which Jacksonville faculty have been involved extends beyond particular occasions and uses. Susan Hill, coordinator of the Center for the Advancement of Teaching and Learning, notes, "Cases have been the route to the kind of scholarship that this faculty enjoys and cares about. They have helped us realize the expertise that faculty on this campus have, and given us a vehicle for sharing it with others. That's very rewarding."

Seven Lessons for Case Writing on Your Campus

Value the process. Both of the ventures recounted above have been highly productive; both groups produced a finished set of cases. But it's notable that both groups saw the process itself, apart from final products, as valuable — as a chance to identify issues of common concern, exchange ideas, share problems, and evaluate strategies for improvement, establishing along the way a sense of community that is all too rare for teachers on most campuses. Case writing is not something you undertake simply to produce cases, these two ventures tell us; it's a way of opening the classroom door, of making teaching a more public, collaborative enterprise.

Set aside time and space for people to work together. It's possible, after some initial orientation, for faculty to go to their offices and write cases quite independently. But such a strategy not only misses out on the community-making benefit of the process, it's also unlikely to produce the best cases. One of the clear lessons of the ventures described in this chapter is that it's in the talking together, the reading of one another's drafts, the giving and getting of feedback that case writers get their best insights. Such benefits are unlikely in the rush and press of daily schedules, and it's no accident that the successful case-writing groups featured here set aside time for people to work together — in retreats, day-long workshops, and the like.

Plan to do lots of revision. Veteran case writer Abby Hansen has a wonderful metaphor for the case-writing process: "It's a little like topiary," she says. "You start with a bush (a first draft), which you clip and trim. Then you step back and size it up, and clip and trim some more. If you do it right, the reward lies in finally producing something with real form" (in Christensen 1987, p. 265) The image points up an important insight: Although cases are "real life," they are not transcripts or verbatim reports. The case writer, like the novelist, must select and shape material to achieve the intended effect — in this instance, provoking substantive discussion about teaching and learning. And that takes lots of drafts, feedback, and revision.

Connect cases to existing faculty concerns and interests. Cases are most likely to have an impact when they're connected to other teaching-improvement activities. If, for instance, your campus has a group of faculty doing Classroom Research, you may find individuals for whom case writing is a natural vehicle for more widely sharing what they're discovering — something K. Patricia Cross has found that CR practitioners *want* to do. ("See You On Wednesday!" in Chapter III, might be a model for such cases.) Case writing also might provide a center of gravity for mentoring relationships: Having a new faculty member observe a more experienced colleague's class, review course materials, and interview students would not only be appropriate "research" for a case the two could collaborate in developing, it would give purpose and focus to the mentoring relationship itself.

Think about incentives and rewards. Neither Florida Community College at Jacksonville nor the Washington Center provided any financial stipend or release time to faculty who were writing cases. What faculty *did* get was a sense of colleagueship and community, occasional technical assistance, and lots of moral support. Even more important, they got a degree of professional recognition, as their cases were printed (albeit in fairly rough-and-ready form) and disseminated. It's worth noting, in the spirit of incentives and rewards, that there are now several national outlets for cases. James Rhem, editor of *The National Teaching & Learning Forum*, a newsletter for college faculty, has begun a regular case feature: a case with commentary by two faculty readers. The journal of the Professional and Organizational Development (POD) Network, *To Improve the Academy*, recently ran several cases with suggestions from their authors of how the cases might be used (Volume 11, 1992). The next step is to get the disciplines on board, with cases about the teaching of a particular field successfully competing with other forms of scholarly writing for a place in prestigious disciplinary journals. The point is that campuses seeking to develop cases might well think about such possible outlets; publication is a highly relevant reward for faculty who develop cases and one of the steps on the way to a more scholarly view of teaching itself.

Address issues of confidentiality and ethics (before a problem arises). Case writing almost instantly raises tricky issues about what should and should not be public — about students, colleagues, the campus, oneself. Jacksonville's Susan Hill notes, "We're not sure we figured out all these issues of confidentiality once and for all, but you can't just pretend they're not there. It's a subject you have to discuss." You also might want to track down a useful piece by Judith Kleinfeld (1990), "Ethical Issues and Legal Liability in Writing Cases About Teaching."

Don't make it harder than it needs to be. Case writing, like case-discussion facilitation, is not a sacred mystery. Your campus probably has lots of relevant expertise — sometimes in places you don't expect to find it. There are useful things to read. But follow your instincts, revise and then revise some more, try your case with an audience, and revise once more.

CHAPTER V

ACHIEVING THE PROMISE OF CASES
Next Steps and Emerging Issues

The use of cases to improve teaching is at an early stage of development; much remains to be learned about what works, for what purposes, and how well. Nevertheless, it's possible to say something about the questions that need to be addressed in the next phase of activity.

How Can Cases Put the Focus on Learning As Well as Teaching?

Many of the cases that are currently available focus primarily on the experience of the teacher; typically, the action is seen through a teacher's eyes, and it is with the teacher that the reader is invited to identify. Teacher-focused cases are all to the point if what you want is a discussion of teaching. What such cases might not do is to get people's attention on *learning* — or on the connection *between* teaching and learning that K. Patricia Cross has been urging us to attend to for several years now. For that, we need cases that focus on the student's (or students') experience, not just the teacher's; cases that report not only how the teacher thinks and behaves but what students are learning as a consequence.

What would such cases look like? One suggestive model for such cases is *A Private Universe*, an eighteen-minute videotape produced through Project Star, at Harvard University (to order, call Pyramid Film and Video toll-free at 1/800/421-2304). The tape begins with Harvard students, at graduation, all in gowns, one after another interviewed by a roving reporter about why the seasons change. Each graduate is eloquent, self-confident . . . and wrong: The Sun gets closer to or farther from the Earth, students say. The rest of the tape then explores how such fundamental errors can persist, even among the brightest students in the best educational settings, by taking us through the *case* of Heather, a bright ninth grader who also misunderstands.

What we see, as she talks on camera and manipulates a model of the universe, and in comments from her teacher, is the power of early misconceptions to distort subsequent learning. Somewhere along the line, Heather was, we learn, on the wrong page (both literally and metaphorically) and came to believe that the Earth revolves around the Sun in a figure eight; bright young woman that she is, she then proceeds to force subsequent information and new facts to fit that prior misconception. Years later, upon graduation from college, Heather still is likely to carry that misconception, the tape shows us clearly.

It was a staff person from the American Association for the Advancement of Science who passed a copy of *A Private Universe* along to me, and it came with a plea: What we need, he said, are analogous cases at the college level: cases about *learning*, cases that open windows on how students process and make sense (or nonsense) of new information.

Several of the cases reproduced in this monograph take at least a step toward such a focus on student learning: "See You On Wednesday!" (in Chapter III) includes information about students' expectations for learning in a writing class; "The Good Family" (in Additional Cases in the Appendix) includes an actual student paper. Other student-focused cases in AAHE's files include material from student logs, interviews, course examinations, and assessment.

An additional intriguing possibility for getting the focus on learning as well as teaching was suggested by Patricia Spacks, chair of the English department at the University of Virginia. Develop cases, Spacks advised us, that aren't simply the teacher's story, but are the stories of several students, as well — Rashomon-like cases, with multiple points of view. I've since experimented with that model, using an English course at UVa as my laboratory; sure enough, the multiple voices of the case raise issues about the relationship between teaching and learning that are complex and subtle.

Whatever the method for getting learning into cases, the point is this: Teaching is not just performance or classroom management; it's a complex activity aimed at a complex outcome — student learning. Without information about how *students* experience the educational process, what meaning *they* make of it, what learning *they* pull out, cases miss a crucial pedagogical question: Is the teaching here leading to learning?

Are There "Alternative" Forms or Formats That Will Make Cases Most Powerful?

The first chapter in this monograph reports that cases work when they're believable, concrete, story-like, and open-ended. But beyond those basic characteristics, there's plenty of room — and need — for variety and invention. The reigning model is probably that of the business school case — a real-life, story-like account that ends with a "What-should-Dr.-Doe-do?" kind of question. AAHE's file of faculty-authored cases includes many that follow this model, but also cases written as plays or dialogues, cases organized around student work samples, and cases with multiple, Rashomon-like narratives. And while most cases are in print form, there are people experimenting with cases on video and interactive laser disk.

Moreover, it might well be that cases need to differ by discipline. Several economists told us, only slightly tongue-in-cheek, "If you want economists to be engaged by cases, then you need to include some quadratic equations." Similarly, a faculty member who was writing cases about the teaching of math said of my literature case "Tried and True" (in Additional Cases in the Appendix), "It's too smooth, too much like a short story." Alternative case forms and formats should be encouraged at every turn, as should the "packaging" of cases with background readings, follow-up commentary, and the like. Only with such variety at hand will we be able to learn which cases work best for which audiences and purposes.

How Can Cases Get at More Subtle Issues of Practice?

After a case discussion during an AAHE workshop, one faculty participant commented, "This case made for lively discussion, but it's not about the kinds of problems *I* struggle with after twenty years in the classroom." If cases are to engage more experienced teachers, she told the group, they need to focus not on "stupid mistakes" but on the "more subtle judgments and hard choices" that even the best teachers struggle with.

What does this mean for a next stage in the evolution of cases? It might mean that we need cases that have seasoned, self-reflective teachers as protagonists, as we see in "Whose Agenda?" a case about collaborative learning (in Additional Cases in the Appendix), in which the teacher might not achieve his every aim but is nevertheless purposeful and reflective about the decisions he makes. It might mean cases that focus not on dramatic blunders and stupid mistakes but on how the teacher *thinks through* pedagogical issues and choices. It might mean — to recall an earlier point — Rashomon-like cases where the form itself enacts the impossibility of simple, single points of view and solutions. In short, we need cases that represent the complexity and nuance of what experienced teachers think and do in the classroom.

How Can Cases Get Beyond Problems To the Problematic?

The metaphor for the classroom behind many cases would seem to be that of classical drama, with an exposition leading up to some dramatic moment of clash or conflict or reversal of fortunes. But the fact is that many classrooms feel a whole lot more like *Waiting for Godot* than *Oedipus Rex*. Things just sort of go along. As one of my colleagues at AAHE put it, "there's a lot of cruise control" during the course of a semester.

Indeed, the "problem" many faculty experience most persistently is not the dramatic incident demanding resolution but more one of deciding whether things are okay, whether "it's working." As we continue to explore and develop cases, then, an interesting avenue might be to move beyond the dramatic and look more closely at the mundane. Such a shift would turn case discussion from problem solving to meaning making, and tap into a deeper kind of practitioner knowledge.

> "The situations of practice are not problems to be solved but problematic situations characterized by uncertainty, disorder, and indeterminacy."
>
> *(Schön 1983, p. 16)*

How Can Cases Represent Best Practice — Or Can They?

One of the questions that often arises about cases and their use for improving teaching is about "exemplary practice." "Why look only at things that go wrong?" some faculty ask. "Let's look at models of how to do it well." There's a right idea here, one related to earlier points about the appeal of cases to more experienced, sophisticated teachers and the need to get "beyond problems to the problematic." But the capacity of cases to represent exemplary practice, to set forth models to emulate, is complicated by two circumstances.

The first is that such cases are unlikely to "work." They're unlikely, that is, to prompt the kind of lively, engaged discussion that cases are known for. Most of us keep turning the pages of a novel because of its evolving sense of tension, conflict, dissonance; the prospect of the perfect hero moving smoothly through the world is a bit of a bore. So with cases: What engages and prompts reflection is not perfection but the experience of the problematic, the jarring, the not-quite-right.

The second point against cases of exemplary teaching is that developing them can be an exercise in futility. The case I might write about an exemplary approach to teaching *Hamlet* could well seem quite otherwise to my English department colleague down the hall; he has different ideas about how the play should be handled. Lee Shulman notes, "Cases may be crafted and organized as exemplars of particular principles, maxims, or moral visions. But once apprehended and interpreted by their readers, cases can and will come to exemplify other ideas, attitudes, and practices, as well. They are thus no different from any other literary creation. The author's intentions and the reader's constructions are rarely identical" (Shulman 1992, p. 6). Examined by a room full of faculty, just about any instance of teaching is going to show some hairline cracks, and it's precisely the opportunity to probe those cracks that makes cases engaging.

How Can We Get Content More Firmly Into the Picture?

It is perhaps indicative of how teaching currently is "constructed" that most faculty who put their hand to case writing write about issues of process, particularly about the interpersonal and classroom-management dimensions of teaching: How to handle the difficult student. What to do when plagiarism rears its head. How to assign grades when students are required to work in teams.

These are real issues that warrant serious conversation. But, we also need to talk about the "stuff" that's being taught, the disciplinary or subject-matter concepts that students are expected to learn. We need cases about how to help students like Heather in the videotape case *A Private Universe* free themselves from misconceptions that impede learning. We need cases like the one recently developed by Kathleen Quinlan, research assistant at Stanford University, depicting how a teaching assistant in a large human biology class uses metaphor (an elaborate, carefully worked-out account of a "building community") to help students review the concept of DNA replication for the midterm. The case raises a variety of cross-cutting pedagogical issues, but its particular contribution is to raise issues of content, as it clearly did for a biologist who responded to the case by saying, "This is one of the hardest concepts to help students understand. . . . You try every analogy under the sun to help students get the big picture, because otherwise you're talking a lot of jargon. . . . But in this case, you see a teacher get carried away building such an analogy. There is more than ample anthropomorphization here — too much, in my opinion. There isn't nearly as much intent to what cells do as this kind of metaphor would imply. . ." (Louis Albert, AAHE, private communication).

Cases that focus on content might not, it's true, be accessible to all audiences in the same way (biologists can obviously discuss a case about teaching DNA replication in a way that most philosophers cannot), but subject-specific accounts of teaching have the considerable advantage of engaging faculty who might not care all that much about teaching in general but care deeply about their field and how to represent it.

How Might Cases Build on One Another In Useful Ways?

Interesting issues arise in the discussion of *one* case about teaching DNA replication (or *Hamlet*, or the concept of social stratification), but having a *set* of cases on such topics would further enrich the discussion. Consider, for instance, two or three companion cases to Kathleen Quinlan's, cases in which alternative metaphors were employed and the consequences played out. Lee Shulman proposes such a strategy as a way to get at the more mundane but important aspects of teaching: Cases can, he suggests, be used in "contrasting pairs: two distinctive approaches to opening the school year, a couple of different ways to teach *Moby Dick*, or the concept of natural selection" (1992, p. 18).

Indeed, the exercise of identifying the key concepts, abilities, and values of each discipline or field, the ones students can't progress without, would not only permit the development of sets of mutually illuminating cases, it would be a valuable exercise in itself, a step toward a curriculum of college-level teaching that might shape TA training in the disciplines, for instance.

What Kinds of Occasions Are Needed To Take Advantage of the Power of Cases?

One of the frustrations of cases is that the existing occasions for talking about teaching on most campuses are inadequate to the potential in cases. Mostly, those occasions are brief and highly episodic; there's the once-a-semester two-hour workshop and the monthly five-minute brown-bag lunch. Cases that will fit these occasions are necessarily brief and probably not very complex. They need to be read and processed and discussed on the spot, making many of the more ambitious agendas presented in this chapter impossible.

The up side of this frustration is that cases can help call into question the institutional structures and practices commonly aimed at in the improvement of teaching. The notion that cases might focus on issues of content as well as process, for instance, throws into relief the fact that "faculty development" is mostly delivered to groups of faculty from a variety of disciplines, with little attention to the particulars of teaching physics as opposed to accounting. And the longer, more complex cases that are likely to result when information about student learning is included soon run up against the fact that most formal faculty-development occasions are relatively brief. The prospect of twelve-, fifteen-, or twenty-page cases, no matter how provocative they are, is often met with cries that "faculty will never read something that long!" But an alternative and more productive response might be to think of cases as a way to begin changing and challenging some of the givens of "faculty-development" policy and practice, looking for new occasions, focusing less on individuals and more on departments and other units.

What Can Be Said About the Impact Of Case Use on Teaching Improvement?

Evaluating any teaching-improvement effort is tricky business. For one thing, it's hard to know what teachers actually do behind the closed doors of their classrooms; for another, the student learning that's ultimately at issue is hard to measure and not neatly, causally related to how teachers behave.

Still, we need to begin looking at the actual *impact* of cases — whether they improve teaching *and* learning, in what ways, and under what conditions.

Some inferences related to these questions can be drawn from research on cases in teacher-education settings. Two studies by Judith Kleinfeld, professor of education at the University of Alaska, are promising. Kleinfeld (1991a) found that teacher-education students who were taught through the case method (compared with those in a section that employed substantial discussion but not about cases) showed significant gains when it came to analyzing complex pedagogical situations. She also found that novice teachers who were engaged in *writing* cases became more sophisticated in their thinking about teaching: They began with conceptual maps that were "rigid, simplistic, and implicit" and ended with maps that were "much more complex, contextual, and explicit" (1991b, p. 2).

Similar findings are reported by Judith Shulman, research associate at the Far West Laboratory for Educational Research and Development and editor of several volumes of cases by elementary and high school teachers. She says, "Participants in these workshops [where cases were used to develop teaching skills] uniformly report that they enjoy reading and discussing the accounts of other teachers. They feel that they are not alone with their problems and can analyze and reflect on their own practice in a 'safe setting' with others who share their concerns. Some teachers report that they have actually changed some of their teaching strategies as a result of reading and analyzing the cases" (Shulman 1990, p. 76).

Evaluations of case use in higher education settings are harder to come by. So far, the data focus mostly on participants' level of satisfaction (it's high) immediately following a case discussion; there are no reported studies of effects on teaching itself, much less on student learning.

A next step, therefore, for those seeking to advance the use of cases for faculty development, is to develop more comprehensive evaluation strategies, looking at longer-term effects and getting clear where the most important effects are likely to kick in — not, it seems to me, in the application of techniques in the classroom, but in new ways of framing problems, new attitudes toward teaching, and the existence of a richer, wider conversation about it on campus.

CHAPTER VI

CASES AND CAMPUS CULTURE

This monograph argues that cases can help "change the culture," to make campuses more invitational to serious, sustained attention to the quality of teaching and learning. But how would such a culture look? And where would cases fit in?

It seems appropriate to use this final chapter to set forth campus scenarios involving cases that suggest what such a culture might look like a few years down the road . . . images, if you will, at which to aim our efforts. Here are three.

Scenario I: Cases to Prompt Departmental Conversation

For lots of faculty in the math department at Midwest State University, academe was not quite what they'd once imagined. More and more students were arriving underprepared; teaching them was time-and energy-consuming, and hard! "I used to think of myself as a good teacher," mused Dr. George Borowski, "but students today need something I'm not sure how to give." George was not the only faculty member finding himself in that boat; frustration was the prevailing note in hallway conversation, and beyond frustration, silence. "We just weren't talking to each other much anymore," says department chair Susan Roth, "I knew something had to change."

What to do? One fall, during the usual Wednesday afternoon department meeting, Susan decided to try something different: She asked two faculty who were teaching developmental math to talk with the group about their classes that day. The conversation began awkwardly; no one was quite sure how to respond or what to say. But by the end of the hour, it was clear that something good was happening. People were leaning forward in their chairs, listening, offering ideas, telling about their own classes, their own stories. Rather than frustration and despair, there was curiosity and problem solving in the air. When Susan asked George whether he'd be willing to share a story about his Calculus II class at the next meeting, the idea was met with enthusiasm.

Today, two years later, regular faculty reports on teaching are a routine part of department business. Faculty take turns presenting an incident, problem, or intriguing scenario for discussion by their colleagues. The point is to find "solutions" where they're needed, but also, as Susan tells new faculty, "to exercise our collective teaching intelligence."

The discussions have become more systematic over time, with a kind of protocol evolving: "It reminds me of grand rounds in a hospital," remarked one new department member. "Each of us is responsible for presenting a case for group analysis and debriefing." Recently, some faculty have taken to writing up their stories and passing them around in advance to help people prepare for the discussion, which has given Susan and several others an idea. This year's project, she says with a smile, is to begin collecting the department's "teaching cases," along with a brief report of discussion about them, and "assembling a sort of departmental teaching archive we can use as an ongoing resource."

Scenario II:
Cases to Prepare Graduate Students to Teach

Private Ivy University had long claimed to value teaching, and its faculty had always felt undergraduate education to be a first priority. But it was only within the past few years that the teaching abilities of graduate students had become an issue. At first, it was mainly a matter of language skills: Many TAs were not native speakers of English. But Ray Lapin, director of the university's Center for Learning and Teaching Excellence, quickly seized the day and recruited pilot departments for a project to examine and nurture the development of all TAs. "This is not about correcting defects," Ray told a meeting of deans and chairs, "it's about undergraduate quality and the future of the professoriate."

Following that meeting, Ray began working with a set of departments determined to take more responsibility for developing TAs as teachers. He was excited about new mentoring programs in the sciences and about the development of teaching portfolios by TAs in the writing program.

But really intriguing was the new College Teaching Seminar in the anthropology department. "It's actually pretty obvious," Josephine Baxter, the faculty member who had stepped forward to teach the seminar, explained to Ray. "We study teaching in the seminar the same way we study many things in this discipline — through detailed case study, 'thick description,' if you will. TAs work in pairs to develop cases about their teaching; that means observing each other's classes, studying course materials, interviewing students, and so forth. The finished cases then are presented to the rest of the seminar for discussion, analysis, and problem solving." "Eventually," Josephine added, "I'd like to see TAs working with their advisors on these cases, but I guess that's down the line a ways."

Ray shook Josephine's hand, thanked her for "the tour of the seminar," and headed back toward his office. On the way he stopped in to see a friend in the history department. "Hey, Marie," he said, poking his head in her office door. "What's up?"

Marie looked up with a smile. "Great timing, Ray. Look at this thing I've got here . . . it's a case written by one of my graduate students who happens (he's very interdisciplinary) to be teaching in the anthropology department and taking a new teaching seminar they're offering. It's fascinating. What would you think about the history department doing something like this? Or what if I invited my student to do a case about one of *my* classes?" Ray grinned. "Let's go have lunch, Marie."

Scenario III:
Cases as Scholarship in the Discipline

Professor Janet Mulvany is sitting at her desk at Research University, amazed at the stack of manuscripts her assistant had just delivered . . . nearly fifty submissions for the new feature in the journal Janet edits for her disciplinary association. By mandate from her editorial advisory board (reached, albeit, after much hair pulling and soul searching), each issue would now include not only the usual scholarly pieces but also an extended "scholarly case about teaching and learning," to be followed by commentary on it by two prestigious faculty in the field.

All of this was a great step forward, Janet thought. But as editor she was well aware of the hurdles ahead. She turned back to her computer and the draft document she had been working on, "Criteria for Effective Teaching Cases" — itself the work of a subcommittee of a task force formed several years ago to undertake a reconceptualization of the meaning of scholarship in the field. It had been slow going, with lots of her colleagues right down the hall here at Research University making jokes about turning ocean liners and moving graveyards, scoffing at the idea of a "scholarship of teaching" popularized in a report at the beginning of the 1990s.

But the signs of change were right there on her desk, Janet thought. She picked the first case submission off the pile and noticed the author — a good friend, as it happened, and an internationally known scholar in the field. She put her feet up on the desk and began reading.

* * *

These scenarios are imagined — and, some will say, too optimistic. But, in fact, each description contains elements of real programs already in place on campuses and developments that are beginning to emerge in a number of other places I've learned about over the last couple years. Their point is not that cases will solve all of our teaching and learning problems, nor that the best possible world is one where everyone is writing and discussing and even publishing cases. Their point, in fact, is not so much about cases per se as about the need for campuses, each in its own way, to find ways to make the quality of teaching and learning a topic of serious, ongoing conversation, inquiry, and reflection. Many roads lead to that end, but cases is a good one, and I hope that this monograph will help make taking that road easier and more effective.

APPENDIX

APPENDIX A

REFERENCES
Sources Cited in Text or Boxes

Boyer, Ernest L. (1990). *Scholarship Reconsidered: Priorities of the Professoriate*. Princeton, N.J.: Carnegie Foundation for the Advancement of Teaching.

Christensen, C. Roland, with Abby J. Hansen. (1987). *Teaching and the Case Method*. Boston, Mass.: Harvard Business School.

Eble, Kenneth E. (1988). *The Craft of Teaching*. Second Edition. San Francisco: Jossey-Bass.

Edgerton, Russell. (1991). "Foreword." In *The Case for Cases in Teacher Education*, by Katherine K. Merseth. Washington, D.C.: American Association for Higher Education and American Association of Colleges for Teacher Education.

———. (1990). "The Teaching Initiative." *AAHE Bulletin* 42(June):15-18.

Gillespie, Diane. (1989). "Claiming Ourselves as Teachers." *Change* 21(July/August):56-58.

Ingvarson, Lawrence, and Warren Fineberg. (1992). "Developing and Using Cases of Pedagogical Content Knowledge in the Professional Development of Science Teachers." Paper presented at the annual meeting of the American Educational Research Association, San Francisco, 1992.

Kleinfeld, Judith. (1991a). "Changes in Problem Solving Abilities of Students Taught Through Case Methods." Paper presented at the annual meeting of the American Educational Research Association, Chicago, April 1991.

———. (1991b). "Wrestling With the Angel: What Student Teachers Learn From Writing Cases." Paper presented at the annual meeting of the American Educational Research Association, Chicago, April 1991.

———. (1990). "Ethical Issues and Legal Liability in Writing Cases About Teaching." Paper presented at the Conference on Cases in Teacher Education, Charlottesville, Va., June 1990.

Schön, Donald A. (1983). *The Reflective Practitioner: How Professionals Think in Action*. New York: Basic Books.

Shulman, Judith H., et al. (1990). "Case Writing as a Site for Collaboration." *Teacher Education Quarterly* Winter, pp. 63-78.

Shulman, Lee S. (1992). "Toward a Pedagogy of Cases." In *Case Methods in Teacher Education*, edited by Judith H. Shulman. New York: Teachers College Press.

Silverman, Rita, and William Welty. (1992). "The Case of Edwina Armstrong." *To Improve the Academy* 11:265-270.

———. (1991). Proposal to the Fund for the Improvement of Postsecondary Education.

Tompkins, Jane. (1990). "Pedagogy of the Distressed." *College English* 52(October):653-660.

APPENDIX B

RESOURCES
Projects, People, and Materials

Alliance for Undergraduate Education

A consortium of sixteen public research universities, working together to improve undergraduate education, the Alliance has sponsored the development of a set of cases entitled *Scenarios for Teaching Writing: Contexts for Discussion and Reflective Practice* (1993); the five faculty authors are Chris Anson (University of Minnesota), Joan Graham (University of Washington), David Jolliffe (University of Illinois at Chicago), Nancy Shapiro (University of Maryland), and Carolyn Smith (University of Florida). The twenty-plus cases (or "scenarios") in the volume are designed to prompt campus discussion about planning courses, designing assignments, responding to student work, and other issues in the teaching of writing. (One of the cases, "The Good Family," is reproduced in Additional Cases in the Appendix.) The collection is published jointly by the Alliance and the National Council of Teachers of English (NCTE).

The case set costs $16.95, $12.95 for NCTE members. Order from NCTE:

National Council of Teachers of English
1111 Kenyon Road
Urbana, IL 61801
Ph: 1/800/369-6283 toll free (ask for the Book Orders Dept.)

American Association for Higher Education, AAHE Teaching Initiative

The AAHE Teaching Initiative has under way a three-year project, funded by Lilly Endowment Inc., to develop cases about college teaching and learning that can be used to prompt faculty discussion and reflection. The project is driven by a view that cases can be a more engaging, "situated" way of representing and sharing the wisdom of practice. Faculty across the country have participated in case-writing workshops, and the AAHE Teaching Initiative maintains a clearinghouse of cases (about thirty to date) in a variety of disciplines and educational settings available for campus use.

For more information and for copies of cases you can use on your own campus, contact:

>Pat Hutchings
>Director, AAHE Teaching Initiative
>American Association for Higher Education
>One Dupont Circle, Suite 360
>Washington, DC 20036-1110
>Fax: 202/293-0073
>E-mail: AAHEPH@GWUVM.BITNET

Colorado State University

To prompt more cross-cutting discussion of teaching and learning issues, the CSU Office of Instructional Services has developed and published a set of cases entitled "Let's Talk Teaching." The cases are used for brown-bag lunches and other occasions intended for discussion of teaching among faculty, staff, and students.

Information and copies of the cases are available from:

>Kay Herr
>Associate Director, Office of Instructional Services
>Colorado State University
>Fort Collins, CO 80523
>Fax: 303/491-6989
>E-mail: KHERR@VINES.COLOSTATE.EDU

Eastern Michigan University/AAHE Project on Cases in the Disciplines

EMU recently has joined forces with AAHE to develop and pilot the use of cases in the disciplines. Faculty in biology, English, mathematics, chemistry, political science, and other fields have begun developing cases and discussing them with department colleagues and graduate students, attempting to prompt discussion and reflection on teaching and learning issues in their own settings. The effort will result in an evaluation of the impact on teaching and on department culture.

For further information, contact:

>Deborah DeZure
>Codirector, Faculty Center for Instructional Excellence, and
>   EMU/AAHE Project Coordinator
>519 Pray-Harrold
>Eastern Michigan University
>Ypsilanti, MI 48197
>E-mail: EMU_DEZURE@EMUNIX.EMICH.EDU (Internet)

Far West Laboratory for Educational Research and Development

Anyone interested in cases about teaching should look at the work that's gone on in teacher education in the past several years. There are, for instance, now a number of published casebooks available for use with students in classrooms and for staff development in the schools. A good place to learn about what's happening and who's doing it is from Judith Shulman, who has published several practitioner-authored case collections and a volume exploring the role of cases in teacher education.

>Judith Shulman
>Research Associate
>Far West Laboratory for Educational Research and Development
>730 Harrison Street
>San Francisco, CA 94107-1242
>Fax: 415/565-3012

Florida Community College at Jacksonville (FCCJ)

Working under the auspices of the college's Center for the Advancement of Teaching and Learning, a group of faculty at FCCJ began writing cases to enhance attention to teaching and learning (their work is described in some detail in Chapter IV).

For further information and free copies of the cases, along with notes for using them, contact:

>Susan Hill
>Professor of Communication
>or
>Betsy Griffey
>Professor of Communication
>South Campus
>Florida Community College at Jacksonville
>11901 Beach Boulevard
>Jacksonville, FL 32216-6624
>Fax: 904/646-2312

Harvard University, Derek Bok Center for Teaching and Learning

The use of cases and case-like materials has a long history at Harvard; that work is being carried forward at the Bok Center in a number of ways. The center sponsors a case-based seminar on college teaching for faculty and advanced graduate students, facilitated by Lee Warren. Additional case-related activities include (1) work with the physics department to develop a case about student learning of key concepts in an introductory course, (2) the development of videotapes designed to prompt discussion of racial issues in the classroom, and (3) the exploration of case-like role-playing activities as a teaching-improvement activity.

For further information about activities and available materials, contact:

>Lee Warren
>Associate Director, Derek Bok Center for Teaching and Learning
>Science Center 318
>Harvard University
>One Oxford Street
>Cambridge, MA 02138
>Fax: 617/495-5132

Harvard University, Roderick MacDougall Center for Case Development and Teaching

The Roderick MacDougall Center, housed at the Harvard Graduate School of Education, seeks to develop and encourage the use of case materials in the training of educational leaders. The center focuses primarily on the development of educational materials for use with those preparing to enter or currently working in K-12 institutions. Efforts also are under way to develop teaching cases for use by higher education faculty and staff developers from Harvard and other educational institutions in the preparation of teachers and administrators. In addition, the MacDougall Center provides training in case teaching and case-writing skills and is at work on a case classification and dissemination system.

For more information, contact:

Katherine K. Merseth
Director, Roderick MacDougall Center for Case Development and Teaching
Graduate School of Education
Harvard University
Cambridge, MA 02138-3704
Fax: 617/496-3095
E-mail: MERSETHKA@HUGSE1.HARVARD.EDU

The National Teaching & Learning Forum

This newsletter for college teachers includes as a regular feature a case, followed by commentary by two faculty readers. Editor James Rhem welcomes submissions of cases; contact him at the address below for guidelines. *The National Teaching & Learning Forum* is published six times a year by the George Washington University/ERIC Clearinghouse on Higher Education. A one-year individual subscription is $39; order by calling 202/296-2597.

To request case submission guidelines, contact:

James Rhem
Editor, *The National Teaching & Learning Forum*
213 Potter Street
Madison, WI 53715
E-mail: RHEM@THOR.CS.WISC.EDU (Internet)

Pace University, Center for Case Studies in Education/FIPSE Project

Just about every campus these days is concerned about issues of diversity in the classroom. Cases designed to prompt faculty discussion of such issues are being developed now at Pace University by Rita Silverman and William Welty, with support from FIPSE. Plans call for a set of thirty cases over the course of the three-year project; a dozen are now complete and available. Other activities of the center include training in case-method teaching, case writing, and the development of cases as curricular materials for teacher-education settings.

For more information about the Center, contact:

>Rita Silverman or William Welty
>Codirectors, Center for Case Studies in Education
>School of Education
>Pace University
>78 North Broadway
>White Plains, NY 10603
>Fax: 914/422-4061

State University of New York at Buffalo

Biology professor Clyde Herreid (whose case "In the Beginning" is reproduced in Chapter III) has been working with cases about the teaching of science as part of a curricular development effort on his campus, supported by FIPSE. Herreid also is working on a collection of cases that can be used *in the classroom, with students*, to foster active learning of key concepts in the sciences.

For more information, or to discuss a case you have that might be suitable for the collection, contact:

>Clyde Freeman Herreid
>Professor of Biology
>State University of New York at Buffalo
>Buffalo, NY 14260
>Fax: 716/645-2975

Strategic Learning Services

Educational consultant Mark Cheren has been working with campuses to implement a "case conference" process designed to support interventions aimed at improving student performance and retention. The process is adapted from "problem-based learning," as originally developed at medical schools; it integrates mutually supported, self-initiated professional-development efforts into the problem solving.

For more information contact:

>Mark Cheren
>Strategic Learning Services
>4979 Mayfield Road
>Lyndhurst, OH 44124
>Fax: 216/247-0224 (call to arrange a fax)

Washington Center for Improving the Quality of Undergraduate Education

A group of faculty from institutions participating in the Washington Center consortium recently has developed a set of cases about collaborative learning and learning communities. These cases focus on classroom-level pedagogy as well as issues of institutional change. (A longer account of the work of this group appears in Chapter IV, and one of its cases, "Whose Agenda?" is reproduced in Additional Cases in the Appendix.)

(References to the Washington Center "Casebook" in this monograph are from a draft version; a final version will soon be available under the title *The Washington Center Casebook on Collaborative Teaching and Learning.*)

For a free copy of the Washington Center "Casebook," which includes a thoughtful preface about how to use the cases, or for further information about the case-writing group, contact:

> Barbara Leigh Smith
> Director, Washington Center for Improving the Quality of Undergraduate Education
> The Evergreen State College
> Olympia, WA 98505
> Fax: 206/866-6794

APPENDIX C

ADDITIONAL CASES
With Teaching Notes

THE GOOD FAMILY

*by Chris Anson, Joan Graham, David Jolliffe,
Nancy Shapiro, and Carolyn Smith*

Most large universities have a number of students who speak and write English as a second language. These students pose a special challenge to writing teachers. Eric Franzik has taught ESL Freshman English for two semesters and has developed a thoroughly multicultural reading list for this class. His goal is to encourage students to become fluent in standard written English while valuing their own and others' cultural diversity.

The students in this Freshman English ESL class were asked to respond to definitions of a "good family" based on mainstream American culture. First, the students read an essay by Jane Howard, "Families," which describes both biological family units and nonbiological family units (such as church groups, friends, etc.). In a straightforward way, the essay lists ten characteristics of good families. Eric gave his students the choice of writing a narrative that illustrated rather than reported on the aspects of a good family. The goal was to have them write an extended definition of a "good family" in their own particular culture.

The following essay was written by Nahomae Teklemarian in Eric's class:

```
                    GOOD FAMILY

    It was in 1980, when my father was acused of helping the
    Eritrean Peole Liberation Front who were fighting the
    Ethiopian government. He was jailed without proof and because
    we were Eritrean. At this time my mother and my father
    decided that we get out of the city and to go to the north
    were our grandparent live and to which we are from. And after
    that to scape from Ethiopia and to go to the country called
    Sudan which is located in the west of Ethiopia.

    After we scape Ethiopia living my father behind, my mother
    was working hard in order to support me and to my younger
    sister. Because she paid a lot of money for us in order to
    get out of Ethiopia, she use to work up to 10 to 15 hours a
    day in order to pay the rent and other necessary things.

    Journey to Sudan was the worst thing that I have experienced.
    Because we were walking at night so that we can hide from the
    Ethiopian soldier. It was a cold month and my mother was very
    worried about us not to get cold and malaria. She used to get
    up in the morning and cook a meal for us while every body is
```

sleeping and resting.

When we got in Sudan border, my mother had to pay another money so that we can cross the border without being checked by police. After we go to the capital city of Sudan called Khartoum, my mother had to find a place were we can stay. She found her aunt who were living there for ten years. We went to my mother's aunt's place. She gave us a one bedroom from her three bedroom apartment.

After living there for one month, my mother found a house keeping job at the local hotel. That's were she works for ten to fifteen hours for six days. Every time when she come back from work, she brings us fruit and some kind of groceries. She worked for a year and a half very hard in order to feed us.

After working for a year and a half, she applied for a a refugee visa at the United State Embassy. Nine month later, the United State Embassy approved our application and sent a later to my mother saying that "congratulation you and your children will leave to the United State next month." We were so happy jumping all around specially my mother was very happy, she had a tears in her eyes. She wants us to live very happy and to be brave when we get to the United State, because there was a lot of problem that we were going to face. The main problem was that we were a foreign people in a strange land that is far away from our home. And since we were black and does not know the language very well, we did not know how to have a friend and how to progress in life. But that fear is out and behind us now. I thank you my mother for her courage and motivation that brought us the light of freedom. I believe that I have a good family because without them I wouldn't be here living happily in the land I thought strange. ■

© Copyright 1993 by NCTE. "The Good Family" is one in a collection of cases entitled *Scenarios for Teaching Writing: Contexts for Discussion and Reflective Practice* (Urbana, Ill.: 1993) and is used here by permission of the publisher, the National Council of Teachers of English. The five authors are all teachers of and/or directors of programs in writing; their case-writing collaboration was done under the auspices of the Alliance for Undergraduate Education (for more about the Alliance, see Resources in the Appendix).

Teaching Notes and Suggestions for Using "The Good Family"

ISSUES FOR DISCUSSION

What are your impressions of this paper as a whole? As a writing teacher, what specific skills would you want to address in this paper?

How would you preserve the student's voice while addressing the very real problems of standard written English?

Should your personal reaction to the content of this essay affect the way you respond to its language problems? Should your knowledge that the student is a nonnative speaker affect your response to its language problems?

What issues in Nahomae's paper might you want to bring up with the whole class in large-group discussion or lecture? Which issues do you think would be more appropriate for an individual conference? Why?

TRIED AND TRUE

by Pat Hutchings

Pam Higgins was thinking about reader response theory as she headed for Room 113. She was trying harder these days to think about how recent critical theories might be incorporated into her upper-level course for majors, Critical Approaches to Literature. Now, however, she was on her way to her introductory class, where her goals focused on more tried-and-true methods of literary analysis — which students would practice today on John Updike's often-anthologized short story "A&P."

Not that she taught "A&P" just because it was in the text. It wasn't, admittedly, her favorite short story, but Updike's piece was one of several Pam had come to depend on in her introductory course as eminently *teachable:* a setting students found familiar, a narrator one could clearly distinguish from the author, a shapely plot that came to a nice clear conflict, and short enough for the kind of up-close reading that Pam believed should be at the heart of an introductory course like Elements of Literature.

Pam had been teaching Elements of Literature at Midwest College on and off for seven years now. The reading list had changed a bit, but the goals listed in this semester's syllabus looked a lot like they always had. Pam believed that literature was one of the best ways known to teach analysis and critical thinking, and she geared her teaching to that end. She was pleased if students developed a more personal appreciation for the stories chosen, but class activities were aimed at critical analysis, not the expression of personal feelings or (a word Pam couldn't abide) "sharing."

This first five-week unit on the short story, for instance, focused explicitly on the elements of fiction; in the first three weeks, students had learned about plot, point of view, and theme. Pam's goal was for students to see how the author's choices about these formal elements combined to create the story's overall effect. The "meaning" of literature was not, she told students, hidden in the depths but right there on the surface in the words. "What you'll learn in this class is how to pay attention — really pay attention — to the words," she had said in the opening class four weeks ago.

Pam's attention to analysis was also part of the larger picture at Midwest College, where attempts were under way to teach writing and critical thinking across the curriculum.

Pam felt lucky to have landed at this small liberal arts college for women. The faculty were good colleagues, who put first emphasis on teaching and students; students themselves were the type that Pam believed she could really help.

Take Sue for instance, who was arriving just as Pam walked into Room 113. If there was a typical student at Midwest, Sue was it: late twenties, a single mother with a young child, the first in her family to go to college, and a bit surprised to be there. Pam liked her students: They were nice people — eager to learn to use their minds in new ways, excited about exploring new ways of looking at the world.

Sue was just shrugging her coat off her shoulders as Pam came in. "Hi, Sue," Pam said cheerily. "Lousy weather, eh?" It was a gray day, the end of a long winter in the Minneapolis area. Pam was aware that if there were going to be any energy in the classroom today, she was going to have to supply it. Everyone was worn down by mid-March in this town.

The room quickly filled up. "Hi, Barbara. Hi, Stephanie." Pam greeted people while she organized her notes and material on the desk. She glanced up at the clock: Her classes always began on time!

"Well," said Pam, moving forward into the room, "we finished 'Young Goodman Brown' last time. I wonder if there are any last thoughts about Hawthorne before we turn to today's assignment, John Updike's 'A&P.'" She looked expectantly around the room. People were still getting settled. Pam waited, not minding a little silence.

"Okay, then, let's forge ahead," Pam announced. "I know some of you found Hawthorne's world a strange place, but here we are in a setting we all know too well: the supermarket! I spent hours there just last night!" she laughed.

"But I bet you didn't see any girls in bikinis!" Janice was just the kind of student you pray for, Pam thought: always prepared, always ready to jump in and get the discussion rolling.

Pam grinned. "That's for sure — especially not around here in March! And those girls in bikinis are what get Updike's story rolling, aren't they? Let's read the opening passage where they come into the grocery store."

> In walks these three girls in nothing but bathing suits. I'm in the third checkout slot, with my back to the door, so I don't see them until they're over by the bread. The one that caught my eye first was the one in the plaid green two-piece. She was a chunky kid, with a good tan and a sweet broad soft-looking can with those two crescents of white just under it, where the sun never seems to hit, at the top of the backs of her legs. I stood there with my hand on a box of HiHo crackers trying to remember if I rang it up or not. I ring it up again and the customer starts giving me hell. She's one of these cash-register-watchers, a witch about fifty with rouge on her cheekbones and no eyebrows, and I know it made her day to trip me up. She'd been watching cash registers for fifty years and probably never seen a mistake before.

Pam believed in spending class time reading aloud. Moreover, she believed in doing this reading *herself.* She used the chance to demonstrate the kind of careful reading, the paying attention, that was a central goal of the course, lingering over the important details, noting and marvelling over an apt word choice, oohing and aahing. She wanted her students to love words and the way good writers put them together.

"So," Pam said, "What's going on in this passage? What's important? What strikes you?" She paused and looked expectantly around the room. The low energy of March was palpable. "What's important in this passage?" she repeated. "What words should we look at? What choices has Updike made here that direct our reading?"

Sue raised her hand and Pam nodded with a smile. "Well, one thing that strikes me is that I just can't believe these girls would go into a store like that. I'd feel ridiculous. They're just asking for it." Pam pointed to Deirdre, who looked like she was about to break in. "I agree," Deirdre said. "But, you know, they *do* that in beach towns. Everything is a lot more relaxed. It's not fair to judge them by your standards."

Sue looked down.

"You both have a good point," Pam replied, trying to smooth over the difference in views and get back to the point. "One of the things this story is about — isn't it? — is standards and limits and deciding what's right: We see Sammy, the young grocery store clerk who narrates the story, eventually having to choose between his job and loyalty to the girls. But let's just stick to the words in front of us for a few minutes. What can we infer from this first paragraph, and especially from Updike's use of language?" Pam wrote on the board as students offered up their observations:

the setting is a grocery store
the narrator is male
he's a store employee
not very grammatical
17-ish
girl crazy
sort of rebellious
very observing

"Okay, good," she said, trying to give the rather routine discussion thus far, the smattering of words on the board, a kind of point and coherence: "We've now established quite a bit about our narrator. And in the first paragraph we actually have most of the plot in a nutshell version: Sammy intent on three girls in swimsuits and, as a consequence, getting into hot water with an older person — the cash-register-watcher. Is there some foreshadowing here? How does this first episode relate to the larger story?" Pam looked across the twenty-four faces in front of her, hoping someone would point to the conclusion of the story, where Sammy has to decide whether to uphold store policy — no swimsuits allowed — or side with the girls and lose his job. No one spoke. Pam smiled. "It's not so easy thinking about summer in a beach town on this gray day in Minneapolis, is it?" she said, soothingly. "Let's try something else." This would be a good time, she thought, to vary the pace with some small-group work.

"What I'd like you to do for the next twenty minutes is to pull your chairs around in groups of four or five and analyze the *theme of the story*. We talked about theme last week, you remember, and how elements like point of view and setting and style contribute to our sense of the theme. So, what theme or themes do you see in 'A&P'? As always, you should be prepared to explain how passages in the story support your ideas."

The groups went to work, slowly at first, but with pages turning . . . just what Pam had hoped for. Several groups were beginning to buzz. The group by the window was leaning in toward Jane's text, which Jane was pointing to and reading from. "Too good to be true," Pam said to herself.

Pam drifted from group to group, just listening in, but making her presence felt, keeping people on task. The point was not to "share" at random but to analyze. Pam perched on the edge of the desk and picked some lint off her corduroy pants, listening all the while. When she heard one of the groups drift off into talk of part-time jobs (apparently someone in the group had once worked in a grocery store), she looked at the clock: 10:40. Only twenty minutes left; time to get rolling.

"Let's see what you came up with," she called out. "Hello!" she shouted, grinning, to the group in the back. "Which group would be willing to start us off?"

A hand went up by the window. Jane was in her early twenties, single, more sure of herself than many of the students, and with definite opinions. Pam looked around for another hand, since Jane had a tendency to dominate the discussion, but the doldrums seemed to have settled back over the room. She nodded at Jane.

"My group thinks that the theme of this story is sexism," Jane announced. "You said to look for passages, and that's what we did. Listen to this: 'She had on a kind of dirty-pink — beige maybe, I don't know — bathing suit with a little nubble all over it and what got me, the straps were down. They were off her shoulders looped loose around the cool tops of her arms, and I guess as a result the suit had slipped a little on her, so all around the top of the cloth there was this shining rim. . . .' If this isn't a story about sexism. . . ." Jane's voice trailed off.

Pam nodded slowly, giving herself a moment to think. "So, Jane, you're saying the theme is sexism," she repeated. "Hmmm." Having taught the story repeatedly, Pam was not really surprised by Jane's answer; she felt like she knew every twist and turn the discussion might take. But how to respond was always tricky — and all the talk about political correctness now made it trickier yet. "Hmmm," she repeated, looking thoughtful, her mind scrambling for the best way to get the discussion back on track. Every face in the room seemed fastened on her. The best thing, she thought, is to let this run its course for a bit, then turn back to analysis. "Are there reactions to Jane's comment?" she asked.

"It's not just mine," Jane said. "We all agree in my group." Others nodded. Nicole, seated next to Jane, added, "We talked about beer ads, always with girls in bikinis. Car ads. I'm just sick of it. And now here it is in class, as well!"

Other students agreed, and several made comments about an introductory sociology class where, Pam knew, the professor's feminist values were openly evident and eye-opening for many of the students from traditional families who were only beginning to think about their world more critically. Pam shared those values — completely — but her goals in this class demanded, she believed, a different tack.

Pam went to the board and slowly wrote "THEME" and "POINT OF VIEW," in big letters. "Jane's comment is a great way for us to think about the elements of fiction we've been talking about for the past few weeks. Let's review and then come back around to the issue of theme and where sexism fits in. Barbara: What is point of view?"

"Who is telling the story?" said Barbara.

"Who is telling the story," Pam wrote on the board. "Are there other definitions we should capture?" The room was silent. "And who is telling this story? Janice?"

"It's first person," said Janice. "The grocery guy is telling the story."

"Okay. It's Sammy," said Pam. "And here we come to a crucial point in helping us deal with Jane's comment — Jane's group's comment — that the theme of this story is sexism. Is it the author or the narrator who's the sexist here, Jane?" Pam asked, starting to feel things falling back into place. (It was interesting, she mused to herself, how what seemed like a tangent could be used to bring the discussion back around, to make a point more forcefully.) "Remember what we said a couple weeks ago about distinguishing between the author's attitudes and those of the narrator."

"But how do you know they're not the same?" Jane shot back. "I don't see how we can be so sure. We don't know anything about Updike. I don't see why we should give him the benefit of the doubt. Maybe sexism isn't the theme he *intended,* but it's sure the one that *I* get. Nine-tenths of the story is a kid drooling over three girls in swimsuits!"

Pam walked back to the board and underlined THEME. "We can call the narrator a sexist pig if we want to," she said, trying to lighten up a little, smiling. "But you make an important point when you say *nine-tenths of the story*. What about the final tenth? Something else is happening at the end, isn't it, and we need to get the whole plot in focus in order to make inferences about the theme." She underlined the word again. "Is it sexism that this story is finally about?"

Pam glanced up at the clock. It was 10:53. Only seven minutes left to set things right. "Let's look at the end of the story. What has happened?"

"Sammy has to make a choice?" Sue responded.

"Yes, yes," said Pam encouragingly. "Keep going."

"Sammy has to decide whether to side with the girls when the manager embarrasses them or to quit his job," Sue continued. "He makes a mistake. He shouldn't have quit."

"Hmmm," said Pam. "Is that what Updike thinks or is that your view?"

"It's mine." Sue responded.

"And what about the rest of you?" Pam asked. "What hints do we have about what Updike thinks is important here at the end? Any quick thoughts about theme in the last couple minutes?"

No hands went up, and Pam glanced at her watch: three minutes left. "Let me ask you to do a little exercise we did last week as a way of figuring out where we've gotten today. On any old sheet of paper, write me a sentence explaining what you think the most important point of this class was, and — second — what we should start with next time, what you want to talk more about. You don't have to put your names on your papers if you don't want to."

Pam erased the board as students wrote. She had, she thought, made the most of a bad situation today, but sometimes fifty minutes just wasn't enough. It was hard keeping people on track, and any little tangent threatened to take things away from the goals that were most important for students like these — to think critically, not always to respond out of personal experience, to develop analytical tools that would stand them in good stead beyond this course.

"Just leave your comments on the chair by the door," she said in a voice as cheerful as she could muster. "I'll see you on Monday."

On the way down the hall, Pam flipped through the students' comments:

```
Most important: Women are often treated unfairly in
literature.
Next time: I don't want to waste any more time on this story.

Most important: Theme and point of view.
Next time: I don't really know.

Pam, I don't really understand why you would assign a story
like this. It's insulting.— Nicole Benson
Most important: You really have to know how to analyze to
```

```
    understand the stories we read in this class.
    Next time: Maybe you could tell us something about Updike.

    Most important: What I want to say is that this was a really
    interesting discussion.
    Next time: More of the same? I hope so.

    Most important: Theme.
    Next time: I don't know if I really understand the theme.
```

Pam read over the entire stack when she got settled in her office. She was feeling a bit of mid-March weariness herself. Her next class, Critical Approaches to Literature, began in twenty-five minutes back in Room 113. ∎

© Copyright 1993 by AAHE. Pat Hutchings is director of the AAHE Teaching Initiative, American Association for Higher Education. Before joining AAHE, she was a faculty member in the English Department at Alverno College, in Milwaukee; she continues to teach, part-time, at the University of Maryland University College.

Teaching Notes and Suggestions for Using "Tried and True"

Though this case was written with teachers of literature in mind, it is certainly accessible to faculty in other fields, as well. And though an audience that knows the Updike story would bring special insights to bear, discussion certainly doesn't depend on knowing more of the story than what we see of it in the case itself through the several passages that are quoted or referred to. The issues in the case transcend "A&P."

One of those issues — perhaps the most fundamental — has to do with the purposes and framework that drive Pam's teaching of Elements of Literature. Analysis and critical thinking are clearly on the educational "agenda" today — on individual campuses and even in national proposals and goals for educational reform. (The fifth of the National Education Goals embraced by federal leaders and the nation's governors focuses on college students' abilities in communications, problem solving, and analysis, and plans are under way to devise a national assessment of those abilities.) Many teachers find Pam Higgins's goals quite congenial. But others find her implied theory of literary response rigid and outdated in its formalist assumptions. The interesting dilemma posed by the case, then, entails a possible mismatch between goals related to student thinking skills and the character of reader response . . . which is personal, political, and highly contextual. Pam tries hard to keep discussion focused on the former: Should she have made greater allowance for the latter? Are her goals and her students' interests and concerns vis-à-vis "A&P" in irreconcilable tension? Is "the problem" of the case a problem with the goals of the course?

Or, alternatively, is the problem not with Pam's goals themselves but with her skill in achieving them? How successful is she? Does she make a mistake in letting students work in groups, with relatively little guidance? If you endorse the analysis/critical thinking goals that Pam embraces, are there better strategies for achieving them? A different way of organizing the class session? A way to "salvage" those goals in the next class session?

A focus on the next class session brings attention to the "one minute papers" that Pam collects from students at the end of class. How helpful are they? What cues should Pam take from them? What, if anything, do they suggest in terms of subsequent class sessions? Would it have been better not to have asked students for their reactions? The case invites discussion of strategies for "Classroom Assessment" that audience members may have found useful — or not.

Finally, "Tried and True" raises questions about how to think about teaching that goes wrong. Pam is discouraged at the end of the case; what seemed to have worked in the past now seems not to. She doesn't know what to feel, we're told, about what happened. Is the class session a disaster? Does Pam fail? What should she make of the student comment that "this was a really interesting discussion." What is the *meaning* of the experience represented in the case? Is there a lesson to be drawn from it?

Does Pam need more information in order to reflect usefully upon what has happened? If so, what kind, and how can she get that information? How do teachers learn from experience? How can we help one another to do so?

THE CLASS PLAN GONE ASTRAY

by Sharon McDade

Dolores Taylor backed up slowly until she bumped into the blackboard. She was bewildered by the discussion taking place in front of her. It was completely out of control, and she had no idea how to pull it back together.

Dolores was a new psychology instructor at Johnstown Community College. She taught basic, introductory courses. Because other, more advanced courses built on these, the department provided her with syllabi. Her first-semester courses had been average for the first college teaching outing of a newly minted professor. Her assigned senior faculty mentor, Dr. Randy Harding, had worked with her during the first semester to sharpen her teaching skills. He had particularly admonished Dolores to use less lecture and to introduce more opportunities for students to practice critical thinking. Dolores interpreted this as a suggestion that she should incorporate more discussion into her classes. She herself categorized her teaching style as academically adequate but not inspired.

In addition to her teaching job, Dolores worked part-time at a local gift store to make ends meet for her three young children. She had taught a variety of basic psychology courses while working on her doctorate degree and was relying heavily on the lecture notes she had prepared for those classes now that she was teaching full-time. The transition to a new town, to juggling full-and part-time jobs, and to taking care of three children and a salesman-husband who traveled often was difficult. Still, Dolores was determined to make her courses important to students.

On this day, Dolores lectured on theories of moral development, comparing the studies done by Kohlberg with the more recent ones by Gilligan. Kohlberg's theory, she pointed out with an overhead transparency, relies on a reasoning structure that "privileges detachment and objectivity"; individuals are seen as progressing toward moral maturity as they increasingly see themselves as separate from family, peers, and society. In contrast, Dolores noted, Gilligan — who focused her research on females — sees moral development as related to (not separate from) one's sense of connection to others.

"How would this difference play out in practice?" Dolores asked. She illustrated one answer to that question by recounting research based on responses to a story about a man — Heinz — who needed money to buy expensive medicine for his sick wife. "Was it ethical for Heinz to steal the medicine? To steal money to pay for the drugs? How would you decide?"

Dolores paused after these questions, letting them sink in for students before she went on. She was aware that this was tricky territory, where dichotomies were all too easy. "Note," she said, "that the difference between Kohlberg and Gilligan is *not* a difference in how the Heinz question would be resolved. It's a difference in *how people think through the problem.*" Thus, she continued, Kohlberg would argue that people at the highest level of ethical development would answer "the Heinz question" through reasoning that had a certain detachment; they would see the principles of the problem as something apart from their personal circumstances. But Gilligan found that young girls queried with the same problem would ask many questions, attempting to find a context. They would try to add other dimensions, in an attempt to understand the reasons for the husband's behavior "by deliberately and imaginatively trying to extend into another's position to understand the reasoning." According to Kohlberg's scale, Dolores concluded, pointing back to her overhead, this reasoning was on a lower level; for Gilligan it indicated a different way of seeing the world, as women listened to an inner voice that drew them closer to their subjects.

At the conclusion of her lecture, Dolores had planned for approximately twenty minutes of discussion — an attempt to incorporate more discussion into her classes, as Dr. Harding had advised. "From your daily experiences, how real are the differences between the ways that men and women deal with moral situations?" she opened.

"It's right on!" exclaimed Rachel, an older, black woman who sat in the front row and was often one of the first students to jump into discussion. "Now I understand why my husband and I disagree so much!" There was friendly and understanding laughter from other women in the class.

"Did this research *not* ring true for anyone?" Dolores asked, attempting to generate some discussion. "Jason, what do you think?"

"I don't understand it," Jason retorted. Jason, perhaps the youngest student among a class of mostly adult students, often seemed to view situations simplistically. For him, the world was black and white, with few shadings of gray. "Ethical principles are just that — principles. They're either right or wrong. What's to discuss?"

Gabrielle was a teacher in the local high school who was taking courses for recertification. She often answered questions from the context of her Catholic upbringing and illuminated her answers with relevant stories from her teaching experiences. Clearly from her now tense body language, she could not let that statement pass. Dolores pointed to her and Gabrielle shot back: "Situations depend on the context. Stealing medicine for a sick wife is very different from stealing drugs on the street. You can't even consider the situations in the same way."

"Are there situations when stealing might be the ethical choice for a problem?" asked Dolores, trying to keep the discussion in control.

"Stealing is stealing. It's either right or wrong," Jason retorted. "Look, I've got a situation for you. There's all this controversy about letting women reporters into men's locker rooms. Is it ethical? Is it right? Answer me this: Would we let male reporters into the locker rooms of women's athletic teams? What do you think, Gabrielle?"

Gabrielle jumped back into the conversation. "It isn't that simple. It's not either/or. Why do the reporters interview in the locker room? Why can't they all wait outside until the athletes shower and dress, and catch them outside the locker room?"

"No," Jason exclaimed. "That wasn't the question. Would you let male reporters into women's locker rooms?"

"It isn't fair either way. Both sexes have equal access. Why does it have to be in the locker rooms? It's insulting that the male athletes have to endure the invasion of their privacy anyway." It did not take Gabrielle any time at all to warm to the debate.

"But should male reporters be allowed in women's locker rooms? They aren't now. That's not equal," Jason rebounded.

"Wait a minute," Dolores interjected, trying to regain control. "This is a good example of the Kohlberg/Gilligan dichotomies. Jason sees this question in opposites, as a logically structured, objective problem. Gabrielle is struggling to find the context, to understand how and why, and to develop an alternative solution that will settle all the demands."

Jason blurted, "But that wasn't my question. Should men be allowed in women's locker rooms? Gabrielle, you never answered. You only equivocated."

"Perhaps we ought to explore another facet of this issue," ventured Dolores, with a pleading note in her voice.

"Wait a minute. I want to know what Gabrielle thinks. Would you let in men?" Jason demanded.

Gabrielle looked cornered. She glanced around the room for a cue as to what she should do. Dolores looked lost. She had retreated from where she had been standing at the beginning of the discussion, amidst the first row of desks, until she was against the blackboards at the front of the room. Finally Gabrielle responded, as if caught between a rock and a hard place, "No, male reporters should not be allowed into women's locker rooms."

"I knew it!" exclaimed Jason, pleased with his victory. "There *is* a double standard!" ∎

© Copyright 1990 by Sharon McDade. Sharon McDade is a faculty member in the Department of Higher and Adult Education, Teachers College, Columbia University. "The Class Plan Gone Astray" is based in part on a case study, "The Mystery of the Missing Master English Student," by Donna K. Warford-Alley, of Daytona Beach Community College.

Teaching Notes and Suggestions for Using "The Class Plan Gone Astray"

Though brief, this is a rich case, full of details relevant to the problem it leaves us with at the end. The case easily will support two entirely different directions of analysis focused on *gender/ethnic issues in the classroom* and *teaching strategies and classroom control.*

A good place to begin is by asking participants simply to *describe the situation*: Who are the characters? What do we know about each that's important to what happens? How would each (Dolores, Rachel, Gabrielle, Jason, other students . . .) describe what happened? The point here is to get critical details out on the table, which turns out to be a more controversial process than one might think.

A second stage of discussion moves to *questions of "why?"* Why is Dolores up against the blackboard? What has gone wrong? At what point(s)? A key element of discussion in this segment will be debate about whether, in fact, things *have* gone wrong. Almost always some contingent will argue that the class has gone swimmingly, that this is precisely what one wants to happen, that if only Dolores could relax she'd be able to seize what is a wonderfully teachable moment. Others will ask (very reasonably) about how students will feel at the end of the session depicted. What about Gabrielle: What is Dolores's responsibility to her?

Additional questions about what happens in the case and why might be:
- How well does Dolores present the Kohlberg/Gilligan theories?
- How does the classroom discussion exemplify the theories of Kohlberg and Gilligan?
- Does the discussion reflect differences of male and female classroom behavior and communication?
- How well does Dolores launch the discussion?
- To what extent does the discussion advance Dolores's goals regarding critical thinking?

Finally, discussion can turn to *the search for solutions*, the problem-solving stage of the discussion, the point of which is not to find the one right solution but to pose, consider, and evaluate possible alternative strategies. Questions here might include:
- Should Dolores have started rather than ended class with discussion? What would have happened if she had?
- What other class plans might Dolores have used?
- What does a teacher do with a "problem" student like Jason?
- How could Dolores have salvaged this situation?
- Is the "solution" here primarily a matter of alternative pedagogy, or are changes in the culture beyond the classroom required?
- What should Dolores do in the next class? Next semester?

WHOSE AGENDA?

by Carl Waluconis

A main focus of the five-credit humanities course at City Community College was learning and ways of knowing. It was new in the curriculum, and ideas of student-centered learning were important concepts in its design. In particular, the course was intended to create an atmosphere of student involvement where students would actively take charge of their learning, assuming responsibility both for the humanities class itself and for the other classes in which they were enrolled. The challenge to instructors was to provide opportunities for students to discuss issues related to their own learning — including, for instance, methods of teaching and books selected for class reading.

Edward Marini was excited about teaching the new course, and particularly excited about his decision to use as one of its main texts *Women's Ways of Knowing* (by Belinky et al.). The book was perfect, Ed thought, for examining a framework of learning and for exposing students to narratives concerning a variety of people's histories as learners. Ed was an experienced instructor who had used seminar-like methods and lots of class discussion for a number of years; involving students in their learning had become a regular part of his teaching. However, for this class, Ed wanted to try to be "quieter than ever," and in keeping with the theme of the course, to allow student voices to develop around key issues that emerged during the semester.

Women's Ways of Knowing was the first book on the reading list. During the second and third weeks of the quarter, Ed told his students, they were to prepare and make group presentations of the first seven chapters from the book, in which the four authors lay out their theory of learning. As Ed was explaining how the groups would work, and handing out a written version of the group task, Charles, a student in the back of the room, called out, "This isn't one of those book about feminism, is it?"

Charles was in his mid-twenties; he had a large blonde handlebar moustache and often sat in the back of the class wearing a long, brown leather coat and leather cowboy hat pulled down over his forehead. Ed considered begging the question and beginning a discussion about how members of the class defined "feminism." However, the question had come at the end of the period, and Ed had a feeling that the class would need some preparation in the form of background reading in order to have a valuable discussion on the topic. A brief response would have to do for the moment.

"This book covers many topics," Ed said in answer to Charles's question. "One of the reasons I selected it as a text was that I considered its applications for learning to be universal. But your job is to test that view. In your group work, as you prepare your report on the first seven chapters, use the time to explore agreements and disagreements you might have with the text. We want to explore what the text means to *you* as we look at its focus on learning and knowing."

In subsequent class meetings, Ed and the students covered other schemes of cognitive development. Following Ed's account of William Perry's work at Harvard, Ruth, a thin woman in her mid-thirties who was working toward a degree in social and human services while going through some tough procedures in court to adopt her ward, asked why a study with such a limited number of subjects could be considered universal. The class spent some time on this point, with Ed agreeing that Perry's "he" did not include as large a segment from different economic backgrounds as did the "she" in *Women's Ways of Knowing*. Ruth nodded as he spoke.

Ed's rationale for focusing on *Women's Ways* did not, however, make much difference to some members of the class. Ed recalled Charles's objection to the book as he watched a row of seven or eight sullen men, chairs backed up to the rear wall of the classroom, forming daily as the work was discussed.

Over the next week, this back-of-the-room line of men was broken up as students moved into their small groups. However, Ed found himself continually aware of a mumbling, troubled mood in the room . . . an impression made palpable when, during what was otherwise a productive small-group work session, Charles raised his hand and said, loudly, "This book seems prejudiced to me. I can't really identify with the examples because it prejudges all men."

Discussion stopped as Ed responded: "Your presentations would be a good time to examine different views of the book from within your group. Feel free to cover both things you agree with and things you disagree with about the book," he told Charles and the class.

Oddly, the group presentations, which took place over several days, did not reveal any of the discontent that was evident in Charles's several remarks. Nevertheless, on the day following the presentations, Ed found himself once again facing the sullen row of men in the back of the class. "We'll look today at Chapter 8 and the book as a whole," Ed announced. "Let's form a circle and have our discussion seminar-style."

As chairs were scraped across the floor to form the seminar circle, Ed felt he was on a tightrope. He wanted to get any discontent about the book out on the table so that it could be addressed, but he was concerned that there might be a verbal flood of whining once that discontent was uncorked. If there was such a flood, he hoped students in the class would address it, since he thought it would not be particularly valuable for him to "rush to the rescue." From their presentations and writing, he knew that some students in the class were ready to defend the book from various criticisms.

With this game plan in mind, Ed began the discussion. "Well," he said, "was anyone bothered by anything about the book? What could be changed?"

Ruth began by questioning the book's definition of family as "mother and father." "Families aren't all like that today," she said. "Today's family structure is not like that of the families of the women who are interviewed in the book."

A few men in the class used this as a segue into the issue of the book being one-sided and not having their viewpoint. Soon, the men dominated the discussion, and the book was being roasted on the grounds Charles had raised earlier.

As discussion unfolded, Ed listened, nodded occasionally, and tried to look responsive — all the while wondering about his strategy. Whose agenda should rule the day, he asked himself? Should he step into the discussion? Had things gone too far? The women in the class were now silent. Some were glancing at each other with a look that Ed interpreted as, "Well, here we go again."

Ed was worried that he had helped to stifle comments by raising the idea of objections to the book. Also, he knew that people in a position of being oppressed must pick and choose their battles — maybe a five-credit humanities class was not worth the effort. On the other hand, he thought that if he handled the attack and no one else spoke, nothing would be gained in terms of students building their own "connected" voices, an important theme in the book and in the class.

The fifty-minute class had twenty-five minutes left. ■

© Copyright 1993 by Carl Waluconis. "Whose Agenda?" is part of a set of cases written by faculty through the Washington Center for Improving the Quality of Undergraduate Education (whose case-writing work is featured in Chapter IV). Like the other cases in the set, this one aims to "arouse curiosity" about collaborative education and to stimulate and improve its practice. The author, Carl Waluconis, is a faculty member in humanities at Seattle Central Community College.

Teaching Notes and Suggestions for Using "Whose Agenda?"

Though "Whose Agenda?" was written as part of a set of cases designed to prompt discussion of collaborative teaching and learning, it raises all kinds of other issues, as well. In fact, a good place to start the discussion, advises author Carl Waluconis, is with a wide-open question about the issues raised by the case; faculty groups will soon fill a whole blackboard with issues. More specific probe questions might, then, include the following:

- What should Ed do next?
- What do you suppose Charles is thinking? How about Ruth?
- What does the case tell us about gender dynamics in the classroom?
- Would it make a difference if this occurred during the eighth week, as opposed to the third week, of the semester?
- Suppose the class ended as the case ends? What might Ed do in the next class session?
- What might Ed learn from the episode depicted in the case?

APPENDIX D

ABOUT AAHE

The American Association for Higher Education (AAHE) is a national organization of individuals dedicated to improving the quality of higher education. AAHE members share two convictions: that higher education should play a more central role in national life, and that each of our institutions can be more effective. AAHE helps to translate these convictions into action. Through its programmatic activities, its conferences, and its publications, AAHE helps its members acquire the "big picture" and the practical tools they need to increase their effectiveness in their own settings and to improve the enterprise as a whole.

Member support enables AAHE to initiate special programs on a range of issues to create effective change at the campus, state, and national levels. Currently, these AAHE special programs are The Teaching Initiative, the Assessment Forum, the CQI Project, the Forum on Faculty Roles & Rewards, and the School/College Trust. Members receive discounts on the conferences and publications these programs generate and can access their consulting, networking, and information resources.

Other benefits of AAHE membership include subscriptions to *Change* magazine and the *AAHE Bulletin*; discounts on registration at AAHE's annual National Conference; discounts on selected non-AAHE periodicals *(The Journal of Higher Education* and *ASHE-ERIC Higher Education Reports)*; and more.

For more information about AAHE membership and activities, contact:

American Association for Higher Education
One Dupont Circle, Suite 360
Washington, DC 20036-1110
phone 202/293-6440, fax 202/293-0073

AAHE Teaching Initiative

In April 1990, AAHE announced that a generous gift from Allen Jossey-Bass enabled it to launch a new program within AAHE called The Teaching Initiative. AAHE's Teaching Initiative is best understood not as an attempt to promote any particular teaching strategy or method but as work on a number of fronts, to help promote a campus culture in which questions about teaching and learning are topics of ongoing, public faculty discourse.

The AAHE Teaching Initiative currently consists of these activities:

Cases About College Teaching and Learning. The first major project of the AAHE Teaching Initiative, funded by Lilly Endowment Inc., addresses the development and use of cases about college teaching and learning. These cases, focused on introductory courses in a variety of disciplines, are intended to prompt more context-specific (and therefore, we think, more authentic) conversations among faculty about how to work successfully with students. This monograph provides an interim report on the cases project.

Teaching Portfolios. If cases can help us understand teaching, the teaching portfolio can help document the ways we put that understanding into practice. A growing number of campuses are turning to this promising new vehicle for the evaluation and improvement of teaching. AAHE has been studying uses of the teaching portfolio for several years and working with campuses that are implementing portfolios. Two publications on the subject now are available (see below). The Teaching Initiative also is establishing a "user network."

Turning Graduate Students Into Teachers. In 1991, for the third time, AAHE cosponsored with several other associations the *National Conference on the Training and Employment of Teaching Assistants*. The conferences are held biennially; the next is scheduled for November 10-13, 1993, in Chicago.

The Forum on Exemplary Teaching. Faculty, identified on their campuses as exemplary teachers and as "teachers of teachers," meet during AAHE's annual National Conference on Higher Education for a special program. The Forum on Exemplary Teaching — which began in 1989 — aims to develop and promote richer ways to represent and inquire into teaching and learning. Faculty delegates to the Forum serve as liaisons between their campuses and the AAHE Teaching Initiative.

Other AAHE Teaching Initiative Publications

Preparing Graduate Students to Teach: A Guide to Programs That Improve Undergraduate Education and Develop Tomorrow's Faculty (1992, 150pp)
    Edited by Leo M. Lambert and Stacey Lane Tice.
    AAHE members: $20.00 each, nonmembers $22.00 each, for 1-9 copies.
    Bulk orders: 10-24 copies, $18.70 each; 25-49 copies, $17.60 each; 50+ copies, $16.50 each.

Campus Use of the Teaching Portfolio: Twenty-Five Profiles (1993, 128pp)
    Edited by Erin Anderson. With an introduction by Pat Hutchings.
    AAHE members: $13.00 each, nonmembers $15.00 each, for 1-9 copies.
    Bulk orders: 10-24 copies, $12.75 each; 15-49 copies, $12.00 each; 50+ copies, $11.25 each.

The Teaching Portfolio: Capturing the Scholarship in Teaching (1991, 72pp)
    By Russell Edgerton, Pat Hutchings, and Kathleen Quinlan.
    AAHE members: $10.95 each, nonmembers $12.95 each, for 1-7 copies.
    Bulk orders: 8-19 copies, $8.95 each, 20+ copies, $7.50 each.

The Case for Cases in Teacher Education (1991, 36pp)
By Katherine K. Merseth. Copublished by AAHE and the American Association of Colleges for Teacher Education (AACTE).
IMPORTANT: Send separate check payable to "AACTE Publications" directly to AACTE, One Dupont Circle, Suite 610, Washington, DC 20036-2412.
AAHE and AACTE members: $12.00 each, nonmembers $14.00 each.

Unless otherwise noted: 4th Class postage included. Allow four to six weeks for delivery. Express delivery available for an additional charge. Orders under $50 must be accompanied by cash, check, or charge payment; orders over $50 must be accompanied by payment or institutional purchase order. Order from Box CB, AAHE Publications, One Dupont Circle, Suite 360, Washington, DC 20036-1110; ph. 202/293-6440, fax 202/293-0073. Make checks payable to "AAHE Publications."